With your whole soul

On the Christian Experience of God

Herwig Arts, S.J.

translated by Sr. Helen Rolfson, O.S.F.

paulist press *new york/ramsey*

Originally published as *MET HEEL UW ZIEL: Over de Christelijke godservaring* in 1978 by Patmos (Antwerp/Amsterdam). English translation © 1983 by The Missionary Society of St. Paul the Apostle in the State of New York.

Library of Congress
Catalog Card Number: 82-61419

ISBN: 0-8091-2517-X

Published by Paulist Press
545 Island Road, Ramsey, N.J. 07446

Printed and bound in the
United States of America

Contents

Introduction

There is no other source of knowledge than experience. (Bergson)

It is not experiences which are important, but rather He whom we have experienced in them. (Moltmann)

Whoever ventures writing a work on atomic energy can follow one of two courses. One can start with a theoretical explanation of the essence and operations of this power dormant in nature. One could also begin concretely, from the crisis situation in which the energy industry finds itself today. Likewise, anyone dealing with the question of religious experience cannot bypass the present critical situation into which religious life has come. Although God is certainly not "dead," as certain theologians of late would have it, nonetheless he remains for countless modern persons the Great Absent or, at any rate, the Undiscoverable. That is the concrete situation from which all language about God must start if it is not to dry up within the safe sphere of pure theory. It is surely not an exaggeration to use the word "crisis" (a "decisive or crucial time," according to Webster) in connection with the religious phenomenon, even though people are now coming to the fore with stylish topics such as transcendental experience, consciousness expansion, Zen Buddhism or charismatic renewal. Rain is never talked about so much as in periods of acute drought. But talk is not the only way to make the heavens open up.

1

Why is the experience of God such a problem for the average person? What are the historical causes which have led to the almost complete blackout of God in which so many now find themselves? How does it happen that most have lost all trace of any notion of God's presence and of God's intervention in their lives? These are questions which may not be passed over if we wish to speak of the story of God and humanity in our time.

Assessing the contemporary religious vacuum, the American novelist Saul Bellow says that our world has become a civilization of ideas, theories, and rational dogmas, and unfortunately no longer one of "sensations and experiences."[1] Whence comes this divorce between theory and experience? And above all, how is it that after the divorce proceedings, we have so onesidedly taken the part of the abstract ideologies while leaving behind and neglecting the sphere of experience? Why so many books on the problem of the existence of God and so few on the notion of his presence?

The rift between religious theory (or theology) and religious experience (or spirituality) was the result of a prolonged process of division which began in the twelfth century. Before Abelard, all renowned theologians or "Church Fathers" had always been great masters of the spiritual life. Their dogmatic treatises never lost fruitful contact with the pious movements of their day. Their theological concepts were distilled directly from their life in personal relationship with God. It is evident in their writings that they were men moved by God.

During the first decades of the twelfth century, theological schools became acquainted with Greco-Arabic (pagan) philosophy and logic. While mystics such as Bernard and Richard of Saint Victor promptly rejected Aristotelian thought, Abelard felt that theology had to be an autonomous, rational, and logical science. It should match the challenge of Greek thought and thus be equipped to respond to the objections of a critical rational intellect.

The rift between this new, modern thinking and theology would be bridged only around the mid-thirteenth century in Paris by the young Italian mystic, theologian, and philosopher, Thomas Aquinas. However, the split between theology and religious experience would again be closed. Theology and piety went their separate ways, with the danger of going off the track, on the one side into sterile intellectual picayunities, and on the other into the domain of emotion and of the purely supernatural. The greatest Christian thinkers have been painfully aware of this schizophrenic situation. Nicholas of Cusa and Erasmus, for example, valiantly tried to reglue the two pieces of the broken pot, but to no avail. Human thought is a living event. A cut-off twig grows, if it doesn't die, into a new tree with its own roots. "From that time on, we have on the one hand a Scholastic theology, rational speculation on the revealed divinity, and, on the other, mystical theology, polarized on the mediation of Scripture and refusing to give any special recognition to intellectual reflection as a means of access to the knowledge of God."[2]

The continually growing complexity of systematic theology on the one hand, and the dread on the part of the ex-monk Luther of all that reeked of monkishness or monkish piety on the other, made of theology and spirituality two separate compartments. Theology belonged to the professional chairs of the university, and spirituality belonged within the walls of the Catholic cloister or in the private subjectivity of the Protestant heart. This break is the reason why the direct experience of God would scarcely come into consideration in Christian theology. But if theory would not be foreign to life, and hence be unauthentic, it must arise directly from experience. "Theory is the articulated vision of experience."[3] Theory interprets and analyzes experience. Resurrection theology, for example, is a reflection on the experience which made the apostles cry out and the evangelists write down: "The Lord is alive! We have seen him with our own eyes."

But if language about God becomes the affair of the theoretical "system-builders" who hop around with dogmas and concepts like an ingenious child with a box of building blocks, then we do not need to be surprised that the religiously hungry person would seek salvation in more irrational movements of the charismatic type, where he or she "at least gets something out of it." Experience and movement then get played off against dogma and ritual, and it is for that very reason that the idea of "religious experience" is so much in vogue today.

Fashionable revivals, however, never last long. The enthusiasm with which many Church people as a rule hail this new "religious need" also appears premature. This interest becomes even more dubious when we see that the very same ones who marched behind the new banner of a "religionless," secularized Christianity yesterday are cheering the loudest over a renaissance of religion today.

There is no more telling example of this than the popular American theologian Harvey Cox. His two chief works, published at an interval of scarcely four years' time, in fact seem very contradictory. In his book *The Secular City* (1965) he explains how modern men and women have to experience being Christian in a profane, rational, adult manner within the definitively desacralized sphere of the big city. They should no longer speak of God with religious, theological concepts (which no one understands anyway), but rather in sociological, political language. In 1969, the same Cox returns to tell us plainly in *The Feast of Fools* that "Christianity has ... adjusted too quickly to the categories of modernity." He bemoans the "loss of the capacity for festivity and fantasy" which has "profound religious significance." He pleads for "religious man" with his typical need for "song, ritual, and vision (which) places him somewhere between Eden and the Kingdom of God." (Are these secularized concepts?)[4] Once again, Cox advises the churches "to play along," this time not with the secularized megalopolis but with the modern rekindled interest in mysticism, liturgical festivity, meditation, and "return to nature," away from the metropolis unworthy of humanity. The Christian now has the duty, it would seem, to join the "religious renaissance" which Cox sees dawning on the whole horizon. Cox is certainly not the only one who shamelessly—albeit brilliantly—carried out this theological (or might we say "sociological?") about-face.

Nevertheless, the experience of God is not a "contemporary" nor even a "temporal" problem. The only "contemporary" thing about it is the fact that modern *homo oeconomicus* thinks in terms of supply and demand. You ask for it; we turn it out. Yesterday, people asked for secularization; today, mystical experience is for sale. However, God does not allow himself to be attractively packaged in a wrap suited to our capricious needs and desires. In reality, the problem of God involves an eternal search independent of the ebb and flow of human emotions. The need for God is a human constant. This need is just as fundamental as a child's need for a mother and father. Nonetheless, this does not hinder many children from living *without* mother or father. It is possible, but it most often leaves its mark on them. A world "etsi Deus non daretur"—as though there were no God— is likewise possible, but it is not natural, and apparently leaves its mark as well, as much for the single individual as for the whole one-dimensional society.

The notion of "need" is ambiguous; therefore, some light on the topic is necessary. Need is not the same thing as desire. Need is born out of the unnatural emptiness of the subject. Desire arises whenever a heretofore unknown object presents itself as fascinating to us. A stomach needs food. A young woman desires her beloved. A frustrated man can imagine that he perceives in himself a physical need for a prostitute. He does not, however, desire her fascinating personality. The stomach's need is satisfied by food. In contrast to this, desire for the beloved is stimulated further by the presence of the one desired. In what sense, then, can we say that there exists a "natural need" for God? Is it a question of psychological necessity, or an insatiable desire (which can only be awakened—and thus come into being—after a first encounter)? Emmanuel Levinas speaks about human love and religion simultaneously when he says: "Desire is an aspiration animated by the Desirable; it is born out of its 'object,' it is revelation, while need is an emptiness of the soul. It comes from the subject. Truth is sought in the other, but by one who lacks nothing."[5]

Augustine's "restless heart" was not calmed by his encounter with God; on the contrary, his "cor irrequietum" was the result of this meeting. Happy pagan Augustine now becomes Augustine the passionate seeker after God on account of this very encounter with God which converted him. What a difference there is between this hankering desire on the one hand, and the empty discomfort on the other which awakens in many one-dimensional, godless hearts a vague need for a "better world." "The Infinite presents itself as Desire. Not as a Desire which the possession of the Desirable would satisfy, but as the Desire for the Infinite which the Desirable arouses instead of satisfies. . . . Desire is desire in one who is already happy: desire is the unhappiness of the happy, a luxurious need."[6]

"The sick person always suffers from something absent," according to Freud. His patient, Anna O., did not know that she was simply lacking a man. Freud at length succeeded in rendering her conscious of the fact that humans are sexual beings in search of partners. The young woman, armed only with this new consciousness, had not yet experienced what love is and what love can accomplish in a person. In our day, there are a few encouraging signs which show that some people are beginning to become aware that we are not only sexual beings but also religious beings; that humans are created not only with a natural desire for a partner but also with a desire for the Infinite. With that alone, however, one has not yet encountered God. Becoming conscious of one's solitude is something different from the experience of love.

The joy in the camp of the spiritualists over the "growing need" felt by many for a hitherto lacking spiritual dimension can seem somewhat premature indeed, because the "rediscovery" of sexuality in our post-Victorian era cannot be called a total success. "They have rediscovered sexuality; perhaps they might also rediscover sometime what love is," Anaïs Nin declared in speaking of the American student world.

They are beginning to rediscover the need for "expansion of consciousness," so one is inclined to muse further that perhaps they might also discover who God is. It is quite true: "Throw out the natural (or the supernatural), and it will return on the double." But God is met in patient stillness and not at a compensating trot.

The sexual need is a feeling of emptiness on the part of the solitary *I*. Love, however, is the consequence of an encounter with a fascinating *Thou,* a meeting which little by little continues to be a "revelation." So also the need for transcendental experience is the private feeling of someone who lives in a too-narrow world. There can only begin to be any question of an experience of God when someone in fact might meet God along life's path. This meeting cannot be arranged or brought about psychologically. If it falls to someone's lot, then it is pure grace. It is a grace, however, from which one can constantly avert one's eyes, because the eyes may remain captivated by the ordinary everyday things and by what is peripheral.

The religiously undernourished person who in our days begins to become aware of a spiritual hunger is by that fact alone not yet with God. It is not at all certain that, in seeking for food, such a person will spontaneously start down the right path. One who has let a certain area (e.g., sexuality) lie dormant for a long time often begins to cultivate the strangest forms of compensation. Astrology, use of drugs, Oriental techniques of breathing or of meditation, the cult of political personalities or catechism books—haven't they all sprung up like mushrooms after the religious sunset over the fallow land of Christianity? The Transcendent One for that matter does not let himself be cut according to the measurement of human needs. The God with whom Christianity is concerned *transcends* all human needs. He does not satisfy the demands of the old personality but creates a new religious person full of desire. God does not bring us what we ask; God transforms us in such a way that we begin to look for what "eye has not seen, nor ear heard" (1 Cor 2:9).

The French sociologist Jacques Ellul shares Karl Barth's skepticism with respect to all the "religious needs" of the natural person (i.e., of the one who cannot yet meet God). Speaking of "the current religious explosion . . . received with joy by many Christians . . . and the new incarnations (of) the religious drives and needs of man," Ellul adds a word of warning: "The process of 'religionizing' Jesus Christ is always the same. It amounts to finding a Jesus who answers precisely to what I expect of him. . . . It is . . . an accommodation to the demands of the modern conscience and vocabulary."[7]

Whoever goes in search of a god to serve as a panacea for human needs or as the missing piece in the puzzle of our psychological well-being will at most find only the God who was already unmasked by Feuerbach, Marx, and Freud as a purely human projection. God does not have a "function" in a person's life. God is "good for nothing," not even for the psychological balance or the spiritual hygiene of the modern person. The "cross" promised to believers by Christ is never good for our natural health. It would be a difficult task to go through a "night of the senses" in a balanced fashion!

In this volume we intend, first of all, to trace how things are in our modern world of experience. Have we really become so one-dimensional? Is it true that in our time, as R. D. Laing notes, "the ordinary person is a shriveled, desiccated fragment of what a person can be?"[8] Is our contemporary faculty of perception oriented so one-sidedly that in fact we experience much less than could be experienced?

If so, is there a positive way or method by which we could learn to see and to experience that of which we no longer seem to have any knowledge? Here it is not only a question of the revitalization of certain thrilling aspects of reality which can easily lose their popularity. It amounts to our opening ourselves up for the entire Reality, with our *whole* soul, no matter how surprising, unusual, and—possibly—less popular certain of its dimensions might appear.

Secondly, *religious* experience will be closely examined. Just as the view which various people have of one and the same person can differ to a great degree one from another (not all visitors get the same impression of the Pope, nor do they all get to know him equally well), so also across the various cultures and throughout the ages God is sometimes experienced in extraordinarily diverse ways.

To affirm, therefore, that all these religions (and, above all, that all their individual adepts) should, in principle, be of equal value would be as foolish as to say that any view whatsoever of a certain person by his spouse, confessor, youngest son, colleague, or enemy should necessarily be the correct and adequate one. People frequently make mistakes about others. Religions are often terribly mistaken about God. Certain persons penetrate more deeply into the intimacy of their friends than do others. God, too, has revealed himself more intimately to certain privileged persons.

One is justified in asking therefore whether there is an essential difference between the Christian experience of God and the way in which the rest of the great religions experience the Transcendental. Only to the extent that this distinction has any relevance can Christianity still make a claim to universality. It occurs to us that the manner in which the greatest witnesses of the Christian tradition phenomenologically describe their relationship with God does in fact appear unique in more than one respect. Therefore it will often be the task of the modern Christian to testify, more emphatically than many among them up to now even dare, to what a wealth of experience each person living in a really human way is ultimately called. May this book be a modest attempt in this direction.

• 1 •

Experience and Theory

1. *What is experience?*

Gaston Bachelard has spoken about "the dialogue necessary between experience and theory." In this dialogue today, it seems that experience can scarcely be brought up, at least once the conversation threatens to deal with non-empirical subjects. In fact, once the frontier of sensible perception has been crossed, strict silence is imposed on experience. The contention is that here we find ourselves in the realm of the non-verifiable of empty theories. Everyone agrees that it is a meaningless abstraction to speak of a branch of knowledge outside the dialogue between experience and theory. It is a dishonorable procedure to deny a priori the right of speech to experience outside the narrow confines of the empirical laboratory, and hence to allege that nothing essential can possibly exist outside that laboratory since experience teaches us nothing about it. It is foolish to fasten a watchdog to a strong chain and then scold him because he never manages to catch a thief in the nearby farmyards! Dogs can fetch objects far flung from their kennels, if we only realize that a dog is not of a nature to languish in that kennel.

Outside the confines of sense perception, there is a great deal for humans to experience. In order to attain what one is capable of experiencing, a person must first have the courage or the insight to free himself from the chain of positivism, a chain which in our time seems very strong. The "dialogue necessary between experience and theory" has in fact most often become a theoretical, agnostic *monologue* within the domain of the exact sciences. Once this domain is left behind, one gets the idea that experience has to respectfully keep silence. One then listens with a skeptical ear to theoretical explanations of a so-called "metaphysical reality" which, separated from experience, can no longer touch life. Experience and theory have been in dialogue about the reality of the Invisible for ages. (It is a dialogue which has of late fallen silent on account of the intrusive talk of a rationalism foreign to life.) What is more, in this dialogue, experience always had the first word. Theory was expected to interpret, a posteriori, the original, living experience. This dialogue, including the religious dimension, must be reinitiated if we want to get to "know" something about the reality which transcends the terrain of the empiricist's laboratory. We must first listen once again to those who have themselves experienced God, and only after that ask the theologians to explain this phenomenon theoretically, or to give it a name.

In order for experience to regain its place in this dialogue, it should not be necessary to develop a new philosophy of cognition. Here let it suffice for us to describe precisely what is expected in the dialogue with its rightful partner, theory. What we call experience is a complex occurrence in which the human spirit and the objective world both have a part. Experience is a meeting between spirit and reality. The spirit "tastes" and experiences something "strange," something that strikes it and draws its gaze toward reality, if not to revise its perception, then at least to add to its view of reality. This is something which, as a result, forces one to drop certain credulous ideas or prejudices.

The spirit which undergoes this experience must give itself up to reality, or at least to a new aspect of it. It is understandable, therefore, why so many avoid experience: we do not cheerfully give up our safe little world of ideas which was built up with the help of theories, and so we close the door. Those who do not wish to experience shut their eyes tightly or direct them toward something more familiar.

Etymologically, the German word *Erfahrung* means: to come to know something by traveling through it personally; to survey something with one's own eyes. The Latin word *experientia,* like the Greek root of *empirie,* points to sounding, testing, measuring. So, experience means to let reality itself come to the fore; to let it work inwardly on one in an open-minded way. In experiencing, one stands open before all aspects of the surrounding world: its colors and sounds, its stimuli and poetic qualities, its self-imposing data and its fascinating mystery—its puzzles, too. In experiencing, one acts like a child: almost greedily and enthusiastically touching and inquiring about the things being discovered (i.e., selecting or choosing from an unbroken "stream of consciousness"). Two motions of the soul can cut off experience, can make us begin to close our eyes. Negatively, there is the already mentioned fear of what is new; positively, there is an ever increasing need for ruminating reflection. "If man does not sovereignly close his eyes," says the poet René Char, "he will end up by not seeing what is worth seeing."

Experience is a happening that is continually in play between two poles: a human subject and an object which may or may not be human. I can experience a person; I can also experience a stone in my shoe. Some people even claim to have experienced God. If the idealists overrate the active role of the knowing subject, the empiricists, who in our day are much more numerous, overrate the role of "purely objective" phenomena which are passively and coolly noted and recorded. The idealist is convinced that "experience is fabricated by the human spirit."

The empiricist on the other hand sees exactly the opposite: "Science is arriving at objectivity through rejection of subjectivity."[1]

Experience is the passive element which is the starting point for all knowledge. Before I can know anything, something must happen which arouses my attention, something which strikes me, something that leaves an impression behind and about which I then begin to reflect. Still, one can never totally isolate this element of passive experience: the experiencing self constantly remains active, too. In each of my experiences there is something which comes from without and something which comes from within. There is no "given" which I can "take in" or not as I please. The experiencing "I" is active insofar as it selects and even supplements material.

From my stream of consciousness, I first of all sort out certain things which have aroused my attention. In any case, I do not see everything. In reality, I see (i.e., I *select* from reality) certain "things." A mechanical recorder registers *all* the sounds presented to it. A person, however, can listen to a nightingale while "forgetting" irritating noises from a distant highway. Specifically, the "concentrated" person is successful in letting go a superficial periphery and in directing attention toward the "center" of what he or she wants to get to know.

The experiencing "I" also is continually interpreting: "When I looked at her, I thought to myself. . . . Only when I got home did I fully realize. . . ." I experience something (for example, the face of a woman). *While* I experience this, I am already immediately interpreting it: her eyes betray sadness. If the experience was sufficiently impressive, then I think it over later on. In that case, there follows a time of reflection. I consider what I saw; I bring it into connection with the whole conversation from the previous evening, with the surroundings in which that conversation took place and with all that I already know about this person. Only now do I fully realize what those eyes were really expressing. Only now do I "know" what I have seen (experienced). Only now will the experience be taken up into myself and become something I *know*. Without reflection, experience is scattered like chaff in the wind. Without experience, however, my thinking becomes a game foreign to life played by a theoretical scholar with a box of building blocks of prefabricated theories. Without experience, the mind is a mill grinding without grain.

Finally, the experiencing subject also fills out that which is seen. When I look at the face of a friend, then I "see" much more than flecks of color and form. I see a person. "If we look at a human face, we see lines and shades, but with it and through it we see a unique, incomparable personality whose expressions are visible in his face, whose character and destiny have left traces which we understand and in which we can even read something of his future. With and through colors and forms and movements we see friendliness and coldness, hostility and devotion, anger and love, sadness and joy. We see infinitely more than we see when we look into a human face." The same goes for the sight of a stone or of an animal: "If we look at an animal, we see directly the colors and forms of its skin. But with it and through it we are aware of the tension and power of its muscles, of its inner strivings which are covered as well as revealed by the skin. We see not color spots, but a living being."[2]

Psychologically expressed, there are various types of experience. In other words: someone faced with a given reality can assume several subjective attitudes. One could perceive it empirically; however, one might also dream, fantasize, meditate, go into ecstasy, or recall something associated with the same reality. In the case of a genuine human experience, several of these manners of orientation are generally in play together.

While John speaks with Mary, he sees her sitting in front of him. Empirically, he perceives her physical facial features and her gestures; at the same time, he listens to the timbre of her voice. Meanwhile, he tries to imagine (fantasy) how Mary understands and is taking his words. Perhaps he dreams about his future with this woman. As he attentively gazes at her, he might suddenly recall a poetic love story he once had read. Her previous words enter his mind. The whole sweet conversation may possibly bring him into a sort of quiet ecstasy. John knows he is happy. It is his first great experience of love.

Only one of these various modes of experience will be taken seriously by many of us: the empirical perception. The rest we brand as being the subjective product of fantasy, with fantasy understood as a childish, irrational, still-immature view of reality.

A decree of divorce is pronounced between the empirical perception and the other, the so-called emotional and subjective, modes of experience. These latter ways are found guilty of an obscurantism which has supposedly stood in the way of true science for ages. This one-sided preference in Western culture for sense perception, increasing since the Enlightenment, is not accidental. This preference is the starting point and the cause of spectacular progress in the realm of technology and material well-being.

The empirical perception is specifically the *only* way which leads to what Max Scheler has called "Herrshaftswissen," a sort of knowledge which has only one purpose: control of the external world. Meanwhile, the world of the interior not only lies fallow; no one even suspects its existence anymore. The split also had a series of other consequences, of which many are not beginning to become aware. Not only is the physical environment becoming monotonous, artificial and unhealthful in this industrial age, but also the consciousness (the "mindscape" according to Roszak), the spirit and the inner life of the average modern person make one think of a polluted wasteland where precious little grows, little can live, and, above all, little is experienced. With the exception of the channel of experience based on objective perception, all the approaches of living reality to human consciousness are systematically barred for the sake of scientific accuracy and a "sober look at life."

In this way, vast, interesting, and essential spheres of reality have been lost. "One-dimensional man" (Marcuse) was the inevitable consequence of this—someone who resembles a radio that can only receive one wave-length. That this person, by means of a finer, more cultivated, more perfect antenna, might also hear other channels is beyond his or her understanding. If anything more is experienced, it is regarded as a disturbance, as "subjective interference," as fiction. That such a limited, monotonous, boring world of experience can no longer satisfy a steadily-growing number of people, especially the young, should surprise no one. The inevitable consequence of the "monotony" is that this modern person will look for with every means at hand, if need be, even with artificial and unhealthful means, compensatory "consciousness expansion."

Pascal's saying, "l'homme depasse infiniment l'homme" (man infinitely surpasses man), is eminently applicable to the spiritually crippled man or woman of today. We could experience infinitely more than in fact we do if at least we would live in a genuinely human fashion. "We protest that we are only human, all too human," wrote Henry Miller. "But if we were truly human, we would be capable of all things. . . . We shall see with a thousand eyes, like the god Indra"—(i.e., not with empiricism as the exclusive channel of experience).[3]

What is missing in this one-sided outlook on reality is not a world apart, existing next to the world of objectivity. It is transparency which got lost, the symbolic character of things which points to something deeper, or what Roszak has called "the sacramental view of Being." For the average person, reality perceptible to the senses has become opaque and no longer transparent. One dares go no farther than safe, verifiable sense-knowledge with only an occasional leap into irrationality after which one is quickly called back to the "order" of empiricism. It strikes most people as totally incredible that the human spirit (and not only frustrated human emotional life) might have the potential to pass to a deeper dimension of reality, to a dimension which is not directly visible to the naked eye. And yet: do not the tears of a beloved person betoken more than mere drops of liquid around the eyelids? Might these drops not be the *sign* of various invisible realities, such as pain, emotion, joy, or even hypocrisy? Is it not a sign that within the invisible interiority of my friend something is going on, something which can only be grasped by someone who not only sees but also feels and guesses what a weeping person is possibly going through? In daily life one continually calls on forms of experience other than the empirical. One "sees" much more than the eyes alone see, though not everyone sees the same thing.

In the practical life of each day, one continually perceives that one knows more than what is seen optically. As soon as we enter the realm of science, however, we can readily forget this. We have been taught to close the eyes of our spirit. Only empiricism still remains alert. The other channels of experience appear to be asleep or switched off.

According to Erasmus, the basic inclination of our human spirit is to try to penetrate the world of invisible things through the world of the visible. Since Plato, this has been the basic attitude of Western culture in every respect. For ages, the visible was "seen" as sign, image and occasion of penetrating the world of the invisible. The invisible is always *experienced* by means of what is visible. It was only rationalism which degraded the invisible God to a purely theoretical object of philosophical reasoning and logical supposition. God is banished from the world of concrete experience in order, at least for the time being, to have an Indian summer in the gardens of abstract, philosophical ideas.

Only two possibilities of knowledge are experienced anymore: empirical experience and abstract reasoning. It escapes us today that, in addition to "empirical" perception, something such as poetical, meditative, or even mystical experience can even exist. In fact, these latter forms of experience for the most part have become lost to Western civilization. We might have some opinions, dogmas or ideas to which we cling, but we no longer experience anything of this world.

To attribute the concept "science" to the "positive sciences" alone is just as unjust (and yet just as current) as to reserve the name "America" for the United States. Typical of this one-sidedness is the fact that classical languages and philosophy scarcely figure in a so-called "scientific" education today. They are considered a literary, artistic, or practical luxury which, unfortunately, do not prepare one well for a real "scientific" career. The speech of a people betrays its mentality. What is or is not experienced is important because experience directly forms the basis of conduct. One behaves and speaks out of one's experience. The poorer the experience, the less human the conduct.

Asked how her son was getting along, a certain mother replied: "Not so well. He is behaving rather foolishly. However, I wish my son could meet a woman whom he could really love; then he would certainly change." The mother was convinced that one who is lonely (i.e., undergoing a poor, bitter experience) behaves in a different manner from someone who experiences heartfelt love. The inhumane conduct of Eichmann, the Auschwitz executioner, can be explained only by the fact that this man no longer experienced Jews as human beings. More precisely, Eichmann no longer "had any feelings." His threshold of experience had become sub-human. He acted "in cold blood." "If our experience is destroyed, our behavior will be destructive," according to Laing.

Christ's condemnation can be attributed to the fact that he was "seen" not as the Messiah, but as a rabble-rouser. The behavior of the Jewish leaders was a consequence of this. Only their blindness was culpable. "Is he not the carpenter's son?"

Indeed, but he was far more than that, and that "more," that "invisible" element, was beyond their limited capacity of experience, in spite of the innumerable "signs" they had been given. They experienced culpable blindness just as Eichmann did. The cold-blooded murderer is someone who no longer experiences his victim as a fellow human being. The result of a falsified experience is a faulty deed.

Christ was thus reduced to a typical rabble-rouser of his time, just as the Jews were reduced to noxious "Untermenschen" (sub-humans) by the Nazis and as a result were treated like animals. Reduction is now the distinctive process of every modern positivist. Just as Freud reduced all of psychology to sexual problematics, Marx reduced history to class conflict, and Durkheim reduced religion to a question of purely social organization. "It is whatever is lower that we take to be more real. The superstition of our time expresses itself in a mania for equating the sublime with the trivial. . . . The mania usurps the name of 'scientific integrity.' "[4] The reality, however, is somewhat more complex. Not everyone is prepared to think one-dimensionally for the sake of technological efficiency or epistemological simplicity. There are people who "see" more than some materialistic prophets would like the masses to believe.

In this regard, let us think first of all of the artist. In direct contrast to the "blind" (hence, immoral) individual, there is the artist, a "specialist in experience," as McLuhan puts it. The artist's life of experience is so subtle, nuanced, and sensitive that the external expression of his or her experiences in poetic words or in material form moves countless people. Those who themselves have experienced life in a similar way, no matter how embryonically, will feel themselves especially addressed by a work of art. Who is more deeply struck by a love poem than someone who is in love? Who is in better condition to feel the words and behavior of a sufferer than someone who has experienced pain?

Yet not all behavior flows from personal experience. The

actor who interprets the role of Romeo on stage does not express what he personally is going through. He speaks words which Shakespeare prescribed for him, and he pronounces them as his director wants to hear them spoken. In daily life, people can also become "actors." They behave, not as they "are" (i.e., according to their interior condition of experiencing), but in terms of what the "director" (i.e., their surroundings) expects of them. They are "alienated" from their own world of experience. They have become marionettes dangling and floundering on the strings of someone else's experiences. Eichmann killed, not because he himself hated Jews, but because Hitler "felt" anti-Semitic and pulled on the behavior-strings of thousands of SS-men. These thousands are not less guilty for all that. Whoever carries out inhuman deeds in "blind" obedience is simply guilty of "blindness," i.e., of denial of experience.

What is it to live in an inhuman world, in a world that tries, if not to root out genuine human experiences, then at least to curtail them one-sidedly? A treats B as a "number," as if B were not human. A, therefore, acts as if he or she had no idea that B is a human being. A has made an abstraction of personal feelings, and, especially, of B's feelings. A reifies his or her acts. In other words, A treats B as an object, as a thing. A acts "purely objectively." This is how A has landed in the world of inhumanity, where no account is made of personal experience, where subjective experiences are seen as undermining practical efficiency. This is "the strange interplay of objectivity and alienation" of which Roszak speaks.

It is inherent to my experience that it is invisible. Only its fruits are visible: my words and my deeds. Anyone who listens to my words and observes my behavior gets some idea of who I am (i.e., what and how I experience). But there is the possibility of being mistaken. I can lie. I can be quite non-committal and say very little. I can control myself, behaving "strictly" as others have prescribed or as an impersonal "etiquette" requires. Finally, I can say what my interlocutor wants to hear instead of what I experience.

The experiences of my conversation partner are also invisible. More than his or her responses and gestures, what interests me is *how* I am being experienced. What is he or she thinking, feeling, while we are chatting? That which most concerns us both remains invisible: the other's experience, i.e., the center of his or her person. "There is no one but yourself who knows if you are unprincipled and cruel, or loyal and devoted; others can only guess about you," says Montaigne. The roots of the tree are invisible; from its leaves, fruit, and trunk I try to learn how healthy the roots are and whether they are in fertile soil. There is only one access to my friend's invisible world of experience: to have faith in my friend. On the basis of what my friend tells me and does (visible signs of an invisible affection: a gift, numerous letters, hours gladly given up in order to spend time with me . . .) I continue to believe in my friend's uprightness. That is, I assume that what I am told and what I observe really corresponds with what is interiorly felt and experienced. I do not act at random, as so often happens between all-too-impulsive people or in temporary relationships, but I act precisely on the basis of these *signs.* Belief is the only form of knowledge possible between persons, no matter whether these persons happen to be human beings or God. Even after I began to believe in my friend who, in fact, became my friend on the basis of this belief, I perceive only too acutely that he or she remains a mystery. Many of my friend's experiences cannot (or will not) as yet be put into words. For some experiences my friend has not yet found the right word. When we spoke openly, there might have been a feeling that for the time being no more should be said. Perhaps my friend was not yet at peace internally. Perhaps my friend could not yet see altogether clearly in the situation.

Indeed, what person knows himself or herself through and

through? On the other hand, we know that countless people carry a load of experiences within themselves, waiting for someone to whom they might express them and testify person-to-person as to what moves them inwardly. But there is no one. They live no genuine relationship. There is no greater pain than to have to "bottle up" an acutely felt experience. What is real loneliness if not the absence of someone who, because of love for me, believes in me? Love and faith always go hand in hand over this delicate bridge which joins the heart of one person with that of a friend. If belief is absent, then love dies too. Love, far from being "blind," in fact gives us the proper perspective for what is most invisible: the experience of other human beings. No one has a better notion of who I am than one who loves me.

I never directly experience another's experiences or another's hidden inner life. I only come to these experiences through the traces of that other person's words and deeds and over the bridge of my belief. Now, it is exactly the same sort of way which leads to God. The essence of God escapes human understanding. The revealed word on the one hand, and God's deeds (creation and salvaton) on the other, witness to me, give me an idea who God might be. Far more than the person whom I love, God remains an even greater mystery. What I can do is to listen to his word and to reflect on the events which happened to the biblical people of God and also to myself. I know that his invisible hand is always at work. "Everything that happens is adorable," wrote Léon Bloy. In the events of Bloy's life, he saw no accidental occurrences, but rather the lines of God's own design. Bloy saw and worshiped God in his works. In the very same way, the poet Guido Gezelle perceived in creation and in nature the patterns of their Creator. For this poet, nature was transparent. Just as much as the gift my friend gives me reveals something of my friend's attitude toward me, God's creation points to the hidden essence of God himself. The only difference is that, with God, false display, conventional gestures, and hollow phrases are ruled out. Any knowledge we have of God is born of consideration of his word and of reflection upon his deeds-for-us.

The dialectic between experience and behavior is, in fact, more complex than a simple link between cause and effect. Every external expression which gives form to content experienced interiorly becomes a new experience in itself. A man who kisses his wife does more than merely express the love which is already within him. The kiss itself is a new experience. The kiss is not only the spontaneous result of his love. This kiss can also heighten his love-impulse. It is a powerful experience. To speak out my inner feelings to a friend is much more than a sharing of what is going on within me hidden from my friend's eyes. This expression in words itself essentially deepens our relationship. To realize that a relationship is deepened is an especially rich experience. If I speak of what I experience, then this speaking itself is a new experience. Whoever can manage to have a free and open conversation with a friend goes home with the feeling of having "become another person."

The expression one gives to personal experiences differs essentially from spontaneous, animal-like reactions. An animal reacts to perceptions such as pain, fear, or sexual stimulation with specific cries and fixed patterns of behavior. Human beings also have such primitive forms of reaction such as moaning with pain or emitting a cry of fright. A human, however, has the potential for much more. We consciously seek for an adequate, controlled, and personal form of self-expression. We operate out of a love-culture which is richer than mere instinct. Eroticism which finds a properly human form of expression is far more than the perception of a state of interior excitation. So, also, belief that wants to be more than mere devotional sensation seeks for sacral forms of expression. The degree to which people give (or do not give) form to religion always betrays the degree of their interior depth of belief. Just as the spontaneous cry stands in contrast to the spoken word, so an irrational trance stands in opposition to the liturgy.

An interior experience which finds no means of expression risks vanishing like smoke in the open air. An affection which is given no form in speech or gesture rapidly appears to have been an illusion. So, also, a faith in God that cannot express itself in a word of prayer or in the practice of worship soon has nothing more to do with interior religious experience. Such a "belief" will rapidly degenerate into hollow theory. Every experience is essentially nourished and kept alive through its forms of external expression. Moreover, genuine experience is always so vital and dynamic that no "status quo" is even possible. What I experience grows or degenerates according to the manner in which I express that experience. No one loves throughout his or her entire life in the very same way. Love deepens or becomes shallow to the degree that I have translated this love into audible speech and visible deeds. This goes in a special way for the love of God, or religion.

If I am creative in the expression of my affection, then my friendship grows. If my interior life takes on living form in personal prayer, then my faith experience grows. If a spouse's kiss degenerates to a conventional gesture and gift giving to a dutiful rite, then the love experience ebbs away just as surely as does a religious formalist's relationship to God. Behavior which gradually gets detached from the experience that originally inspired it degenerates into a reflexive-pragmatic manner of acting.

Finally, the roles often get reversed. The experience is then no longer the inspiration but the expected result of certain behavior. For example, a man may kiss a certain woman, not out of affection, but in order to arrive at a subjective experience in itself. He may give her a gift, not as token of his attachment for her, but in order to awaken in her a feeling of dependent obligation. The rule of life written by a founder of an order—which is nothing more than an a posteriori description of a way of life, grown out of personal inspiration—is seen as a means (a "moral way" or method) to draw nearer to God. Here, once again, the cart is set before the horse. It is not by following the "Rule of Taizé" that I shall inherit the religious depth of Roger Schutz. Carnegie's book *How to Win Friends,* with its directions regarding what is to be "done" and what to be "avoided," can never lead to a genuine friendship experience; at most it can lead to a more rapid association with acquaintances. A certain prescribed behavior can at best facilitate the exterior forms of association between individuals, an aspect of human culture which while lacking in depth should certainly not be neglected.

"Acting" is always the result of "being" and not the inverse. "Our acts follow us," wrote Gabriel Marcel. A structure never produces experiences, but an authentic experience always looks for a way to give it human form. One does not marry "in order to experience something," but one marries "because one experiences love." Whoever feels intensely impelled by a love experience is necessarily going to look for a suitable life-style. Whether this should be marriage, celibacy, religious vows, or faithful friendship is a question of personal vocation. Such structures are not ways *toward* love experiences, but paths upon which a humanly ordered love can wend its painful pilgrimage through this life. It is not the methods practiced in psychology (such as conversational techniques, sensitivity training, group dynamics, etc.) which will lead to a richer interior life, but rather a greater openness to experience. "The expansion of the personality is nothing that is achieved by special training, but by a naive openness to experience."[5]

2. *The myth of the "objectivity" of human experience*

Empirical knowledge is objective "knowledge." The object itself has the final (the only!) say. Here, subjective and emotionally colored interferences must be rejected. The less that the person, the character, and the situation of the researcher exercise influence upon the knowledge process, the more closely knowledge comes to "objective" truth. Empirical science insists on abstraction from the knowing subject. It *must* do this. In doing so, it has managed to record astonishing progress and to subject many aspects of nature to its control. As a consequence, it is all too attractive for us to try to adapt this manner of knowing to the whole of reality.

A person (human being or God), however, does not allow himself or herself to be "grasped" as an object. People who are observed and analyzed in neutral fashion shrink inside of themselves or withdraw. Those who feel they are being watched immediately change their behavior. Taking into account the fact of being observed, they control their natural spontaneity. Whenever they experience being admired or encouraged, they conduct themselves quite differently than when they know they are being spied upon or disdained. When they feel affectionate eyes resting on them, they are in a better condition to do what they would not dare to do in a cool atmosphere. Amid the applause of enthusiastic observers, an athlete accomplishes more than would be the case on an empty training course. Of course, athletic behavior (in the case of sports accomplishments) not only depends on who is following and watching but on the fact that the athlete feels like a different person influenced by the cheers of supporters.

A person's behavior and experience are not purely objective data. They never exist by themselves. They depend in large measure upon two elements which are in principle excluded from empirical science. First: *Who* experiences? And second: In what *socio-cultural* context does the subject have the experience? In other words, what circumstances influence the subject? I speak differently and feel that I *am* different in the presence of friends than in the presence of foes. Every experience is a meeting of a subject with a given object, within a certain cultural context. In the case of empirical experience, subject and milieu are rightly reduced to a bare minimum. It makes little difference whether it is Einstein the Jew or Max Planck the German who carries out a specific experiment. The important thing is that this experiment leads to objective laws which are valid across the board, ascertainable and verifiable by any expert. Whether boiling water is observed in a Swedish laboratory or in a parochial school of Zulu children, its properties remain the same regardless of who or where. This sort of experiential knowledge, however, is only applicable to a small part of reality. It is especially *not* applicable to what concerns us here: the human experience of God.

In the ears of the average person, the concept "subjectively-colored experience" sounds like a synonym for experience which is arbitrary, emotional, and hence untrustworthy. But the average person is the obedient child of an era in which knowledge is considered worthy of the name only so long as it leads to technical control and can be calculated.

In reality, the interference of subjective elements is never to be entirely excluded from knowledge, not even from the empirical sciences. The astronomer doing his observations from millions of miles away is personally excited and feels attracted by the physical object that "interests" him. "Scientific curiosity is the desire *to participate* in what is real, and through its reality exercises infinite *attraction* on the being which has the power of encountering reality as reality."[6]

Etymologically, words such as "perception," "comprehension," etc., point to a situation of active *seizing* or *participation* on the part of an interested subject.

But interference, which in spite of everything is inevitably subjective, becomes absolutely necessary as soon as the object to be known is a person. In our day, people willingly speak of "existential knowledge." In fact, all of existentialism is but one attempt to turn back to a pre-Kantian thought in which there was not yet a yawning abyss between subject and object. But no knowledge requires a higher degree of "existential involvement" than religious knowledge, or "gnosis." Knowledge which originates from religious experience is, in fact, characterized by what Tillich has termed "cognitive commitment." The subject "enters into" the religious phenomenon, knowing itself to be touched and grasped by that phenomenon. God cannot approach human beings as "things" or as "objective realities." God is a person. Anyone wishing to penetrate to the center of a person must first be "in sympathy" with that person. Only one who senses that he or she deeply affects me will lay open something essential of his or her own person for me. A "revelation" is always the consequence of a meeting between two persons who have faith in each other and who trust each other.

3. *Recording subjective experience*

In contrast to a tape recorder or a camera which passively and automatically registers all sounds or colors within range, the human mind goes to work in an extremely selective way to take experiences into itself. A human being concentrates attention on matters of personal interest and concern. Disturbing or unimportant phenomena do not then penetrate this selective consciousness. If someone is attentively listening to a lecturer, then a wagon going by, for instance, or someone coughing in the audience will not even be noticed. Full attention remains with the speaker. To the degree in which one's attention is concentrated on an enthralling object, the remaining phenomena go unnoticed. Some people become so captivated by one aspect of reality that they no longer have an "eye" for the rest of existence. Experience always means "to make a choice." Education and culture play an important role in this respect. A child must be taught to distinguish the call of an owl from the cries of other birds if one wants to train the child to listen attentively to this poetic night-sound.

Just as the journalist who turns on the teletype machine chooses story material from a stream of information, so the hiker retains (and thus experiences) from the multitude of street sounds, advertising posters and traffic hazards only that which appears striking or of interest. The stream of consciousness is continually at work. But it is only through choice that one arrives at experience. A person sorts through the phenomena which confront the senses. On what basis is a selection made? Who has taught us to distinguish the wheat from the chaff? Is it really the chaff that is allowed to fall, or even be repressed? And, on the other hand, is it the most important material that penetrates the consciousness?

What is, or is not, perceived depends first of all upon one's intellectual curiosity and interest, which in turn are in great measure the result of education. Negatively, experience is also further specified by the dislikes, fears, and prejudices which are possibly lurking in a person's mind. There is, in fact, such a thing as a phenomenon of spiritual rejection. Experiences which appear too strange to a person, which do not tally with existing prejudices, are dismissed. Just as education on the one hand can give a person an "eye" for certain things, so also the same education can render someone blind to other types of experience. The Victorian puritans succeeded in keeping sexuality "invisible" for their children. Sexual experiences did not penetrate as far as consciousness, but inevitably slipped away to the unconscious depths of forgetfulness. In our day, it appears to be the experience of God which escapes human consciousness more and more. While sexuality put in a spectacular reappearance after a 150-year absence from what the public considers normal, unquestioned, and self-evident, transcendental experience meanwhile drifted off to the Dead Sea of oblivion. Phenomena requiring acutely honed attention always run a greater risk of being rejected (as foreign to the "normal" organism) than phenomena presented as biologically necessary.

In his distinction between "higher" (or spiritual) and "lower" (or biological) needs, Abraham Maslow noted: "The higher the need, the less imperative it is for sheer survival, the longer gratification can be postponed, and the easier it is for the need to disappear permanently. . . . Higher needs are less urgent subjectively. They are less perceptible, more easily confounded with other needs by suggestion, imitation, by mistaken belief or habit."[7]

Now, experiences come about whenever our limited personal attention is aroused by a certain facet of reality. But these new experiences are never found in an empty, unbiased mind. They always come to rest in an active soil teeming with countless other already assimilated experiences which inevitably color the new ones. The degree of reticence or enthusiasm with which I welcome and experience a new encounter is determined by what I have already experienced with respect to friendship. When a new experience thought to be interesting is received into my mind, then it is first "adapted" to what I already know. A totally new experience is incomprehensible, and can find no "place." That is why it is frequently "understood" mistakenly, in order to make it fit into the schema of what is already known. To come to a changed outlook through new experiences requires a mental effort for which few are prepared. How often does it not happen that a discussion or "exchange of ideas" leads to a readiness to take on someone else's opinion in place of the "ideas" I may originally have defended! Childlike lack of discrimination disappears, with the years, giving place to a series of principles (i.e., to convictions gradually developed from life-experiences) with which I weigh everything new. As a rule, adults manifest an inclination to hold on to already existing thought patterns and to reject whatever does not square with them.

With youth, it is just the opposite. Here, new experiences find a bold echo, but the danger is that they may not be understood, and they are forgotten just as quickly as they made an impression. The thought patterns of youth in all their openness are so vulnerable, unstable, and superficial that generally no fixed mooring is found to which something new may be attached. Often what is new makes no enduring impression; in fact, it may not be understood at all. The greatest hunger for experience remains useless as long as there is no basic outlook on life. In a word, there is no "stand-point." This standpoint, always philosophical or ideological in nature, is a necessary, subjective element in all knowledge. It can be so poor or so hopelessly wrong that a possible wealth of experience remains totally incomprehensible to me. But my standpoint can also become a positive "point of view," namely, a way of seeing which conditions me to "see into" what I have just experienced.

"There are no solutions in life, there are only *displacements*. Something in you helped me to displace myself and I breathe better. Perhaps the old idea of faith?" writes Anaïs Nin to Lawrence Durrell.[8] Perhaps the greatest help we can expect from another person is that we are made to change our standpoint; in other words, we are given a new outlook on the same landscape of existing reality. In this way our world of experience is transformed, as if by magic, into a panoramic look-out. This gift of a new point of view certainly has something to do with "the old idea of faith." The difference between believers and unbelievers lies in the fact that as they both face the very same, mysterious, reality, each one has an essentially different outlook on it. A mother sees her child with different eyes than does a psychologist or a career counselor. What is important is: Which one of the two knows the most complete answer to the question "Who is that child in reality?"

This point of view, this thought structure, is extremely important because all our experiences are colored and filtered through it.

Throughout his entire life, Newman was fascinated by the question of how two intelligent men from the same Oxford milieu, thinking according to the same Aristotelian logic, from the same philosophical background, could so evolve that one could become an unbeliever and the other a Catholic. It cannot be a question of faulty logic or of intellectual dishonesty on the part of one of the two. Neither can we ascribe the parting of the ways to a difference in cultural milieu, since Newman's research was limited to the liberal Anglican intelligentsia of Oxford "gentlemen." Newman came to the discovery that the distinction lay in what he called their respective "first principles." By "first principles," Newman meant a pre-intellectual mental attitude which from the beginning orients all our experiences. Wrong or one-sided "first principles," in spite of the most rigorous intellectual honesty, can lead later to the most bizarre and divergent "convictions." This is why consideration of this fundamental attitude receives such emphasis from Newman.

"These first principles are the conditions of our mental life; by them we form our view of events, of deeds, of persons, or lines of conduct, of aims, of moral qualities, or religions. . . . As determined by his first principles, such is a man's religion, his creed, his worship, his political party, his character. . . . They are, in short, the man. . . . You cannot see yourself, and, in somewhat the same way, the chance is that you are not aware of those principles or ideas which have the chief rule over your mind."[9]

These "first principles" have arisen chiefly from previous experiences. Newman would even say that "the more vivid the occasioning experience, the deeper a principle penetrates into the mind." Consequently, if we want to reflect on our own often very problematic experience of God, then, in the first place, we must critically examine our point of view, and pay particular attention to the unconsciously assumed glasses through which we have learned to view the world. We must become aware of the decisive influence of these unconscious principles over our entire world of thought. We have to learn that no one's view of reality, including our own, is unbiased, but that we can experience only as much as our filtered glasses allow us to. Since these glasses are a gift from our environment, it would do many of us good to consult a spiritual "oculist." Spiritual myopia may well be a contagious disease, at least if we can judge by the growing spread of this phenomenon in modern spiritual life.

In the town of Zermatt, there are "lookout points" from which one can get an exceptional view of the Matterhorn. But in the same town can be found other places (which in fact are more frequented) from which the same Matterhorn is invisible. Likewise, there are life-attitudes which a priori exclude any experience of God. But nearby there can be found other attitudes which, when clouds, mist, and the darkness of night are withdrawn, allow God's mountain occasionally to be seen.

• 2 •

Culture and Interpretation
of Experience

An experience is always ultra-personal, but its interpretation is linked to culture. However personal my past experience may be, as soon as I want to name it, I must call on a word or a concept which I learned from others. No one invents his own language. We borrow our language from the culture in which we grew up. Language is interpretation of experience. First I experience something. Then I try to understand exactly what I went through, by pouring the experience into already-existing frames of reference. "It is impossible for a person to separate a fact of experience from his interpretation of it—interpretation which, except in the case of the insane, is not unique to himself but has been learned from others," said the poet Auden. Among the insane not only is the experience itself ultra-personal but also its interpretation. An insane person may imagine he is Napoleon. His environment, however, knows better and then gives *him* another name, too. The chance is great that the asocial interpretation of experience on the part of an autistic person is a "misunderstanding."

Although we often unjustly consider as insane a person who experiences something highly unusual in his milieu, in many surroundings to affirm that one has "experienced God" counts as an "abnormal illusion" for which modern psychological jargon has a whole arsenal of names or interpretations ready. Whoever absolutely cannot put into understandable words what he has experienced has little chance of understanding at all what happened to him. In the most normal case he could ask a confidant, "Do you understand anything about this? Now, this is what happened. . . ." What do you think of it? What would you call something like that?"

The interpretation of my experience happens in two phases. There is an immediate, direct moment: "I hear the telephone next door ringing." And there is an interpretation which follows only upon a moment of reflection, "At this time of day, it might well be my friend so and so. . . ." Both forms of interpretation are dependent on the culture in which I live. A pygmy who never saw a car will never shout: "I hear a jeep coming!" What he experiences is, at most, "a dangerous and unusual noise approaching." Anyone who grew up in an entirely atheistic milieu will never "experience God" all of a sudden. That milieu affords no words for what may have been such a person's deepest experiences. As a result, the experiences are at best "strange things" about which that person, as a child of our scientific age, might consult a psychologist. Once an experience is "interpreted" by the psychologist (i.e., once words such as "hallucinations, projections, or sublimations" are discovered) this person runs the great risk of dismissing the experience as "explainable by psychology alone." An authentic experience is thereby rendered harmless.

Peter Berger has said that "culture is preeminently an ordering of experience." A certain degree of culture is in fact necessary in order to "feel" that a Picasso painting can be beautiful, that it is a horrible thing to sacrifice living children on an altar to the gods, and that it is sub-human to consider a handicapped human being as an idiot. Nonetheless, there are cultures which see it otherwise: Papuans do not appreciate Picasso, Aztecs viewed child sacrifice as a religious deed and Bantus regard handicapped persons as possessed by the demon. In other words, there are cultures which rank certain human experiences "wrongly." But whoever experiences in a false way also behaves in a false, immoral way.

The cultural environment in which we live "orders" and influences our experiences in two ways: through language and through certain time-bound taboos. An experience for which a certain language has no word seldom penetrates to conscious awareness within the region where this language is used.

Eskimos have more than a hundred words to indicate diverse sorts of snow. The consequence of this is that the Eskimo *sees* several sorts of snow and knows how to distinguish clearly among them while the rest of us only see that it is neither raining nor hailing today, but it is certainly snowing. One unfamiliar with the concept "awe" is not likely to know what it means for a person to simultaneously experience fascination and fear. It is only since Adler launched the concept of "inferiority complex" that countless persons realize that they simultaneously bear within themselves both ambition and cowardice. Before that, these frustrated persons in no way knew how to interpret that vague feeling they had about themselves. They had no name for it. Many of them also incorrectly thought that they were "humble" or "shy." Adler's term, however, made them aware that their self-concept was much more "complex." The new concept thereby made more exact self-knowledge possible.

Before an experience is put into words in a given language, there is only a chaos of undifferentiated psychic material. But as soon as I give a name to what I perceive, I can speak of a "specific" experience that I had. Something interpreted in one cultural milieu as "sexual temptation" (by way of warning) is interpreted elsewhere more encouragingly as "budding maturity" or as the beginning of new poetic experiences. However intimate and individual my ultimately inexpressible experience may be, I only begin to understand it (and, as a result, to experience it fully) when I can give it an adequate name. I do not invent this name myself; rather, I borrow it from the surroundings which influence me. Of course, language is never strictly personal. The community produces a language for its children. This language, with its possibilities and limitations, specifies a priori to an enormous extent how my world of experience will appear to me. Reality appears different to someone whose language is restricted to "modern positivistic jargon" than to someone who uses a nuanced poetic vocabulary.

This giving of a name to an experience includes more than pasting a conventional label on it. The name or interpretation which I learn to give to an experience has repercussions on my psychological attitude as well as on my conduct flowing from it. What I learned to call "sexual temptation" I strive to overcome, to avoid, or to repress. On the other hand, if I learned to regard it as "the first sign of budding maturity," I start to cultivate and stimulate it instead.

Long ago Confucius had already clearly perceived the power of the interpretation of experience. The fundamental rule of his morality is: "Whoever can give the correct name to everything by meditation masters nature." Not only nature but also the course of history is influenced by this name-giving. If I call the political climate of Italy a typical capitalistic chaos, an impasse caused by reactionary fascists, or the inevitable result of too-powerful Marxist unions, the name by which this politically-conceived baby will finally be baptized (in the supposition that it ever gets baptized!) will determine its later course of life and above all the education considered appropriate for it. Here, various name givers are in conflict over their interpretation of the unpleasant social experiences each Italian citizen has had already for years. If someone succeeds in getting his interpretation generally accepted, then he will thereby determine the future course of Italian history. For China, this has been the deep significance of Mao's "Little Red Book." China read Mao, spoke Maoist, and "saw" history in Maoist terms, just as the medieval world thought "biblically" and the Counter-Reformation saw reality through the "glasses" of the new catechetical terminology.

As a result, the question arises as to how modern people think. Who supplies concepts for us? With what "jargon" do we arrange our streams of consciousness? What language depicts our world of experience?

Traveling in the wake of the successful ship of the positive sciences, we have formed for ourselves a language which seems very suitable for understanding material "things" but is totally unfit for describing invisible realities such as the interior life, the psychological relationship between persons (for persons are not physical "things") or human contact with the mystery of the Transcendent.

Now, it is typical for empirically colored language—that is, the language that we most often read and hear in the mass media, for example, that we most easily understand, and consequently in which we are gradually learning to think—that it consists exclusively of "operational" concepts. "Operational" concepts are words which point solely to exterior actions or behavior. As a consequence, "operational" language systematically eliminates the use of words which cannot be translated or construed in terms of concrete, empirically perceptible activities.

"Belief" then becomes a question of "practicing," of doing specific things and certainly not doing other things. Someone preferring to understand "faith" as an interior attitude of openness to the Divine speaks an abstract, incomprehensible, uncontrollable, and hence, unusable language (according to Bridgman). "Love" gets reduced to bodily praxis (i.e. "to *make* love"). Understanding by "love" a state of interior affection is to drift along in vague, platonic idealism. "Culture" belongs to one who has received diplomas, speaks several languages and possibly knows how to play a musical instrument. Seeing "culture" as a refined, deeper view on reality is much too vague, since it is not empirically measurable. "Mysticism" is understood as being the psychological result of breath-control or meditation-techniques, and no longer as the invisible experience of God. Even "God" is a totally useless concept. God cannot be conceived or interpreted in terms of human exploits or acts. The modern world no longer knows what should be associated with the term "God." "God" has become an empty category. All analogous concepts, metaphors and symbols, the very words necessary to name an intangible reality and make it subject to experience, have been excluded from our language. Endowed with exclusively "operational" jargon, language useful only for the empirical world, we no longer have the necessary means to give religious reality a name, let alone to experience it. We only know that experience for which there are no words cannot penetrate to our awareness. At the very outset, therefore, we are severely handicapped in our search for the Transcendent.

Our dependence on empirical language has led to the limitation and constriction of the contemporary "univers de discours." We can speak meaningfully only about things that exist, function, and work in a material way. This is why people call only material "things" "real." The meaning of a thing is further limited to what can be done with it in practice. In this way deeper or symbolic attributions of meaning fall by the wayside.

It was the French linguist Meillet who noted: "The meaning of a word can be defined only as the mean between its linguistic uses by individuals and by groups of the same society." Well, the vast majority of modern people use words to refer exclusively to practical fact. The whole of observable reality is rendered deathly silent, and therefore after a while it is also considered as dead or non-existent. Speaking symbolically means speaking vaguely or imprecisely. "Get to the facts!" But what if God is not a "fact"? In a society in which such one-dimensional language is spoken, entire areas of reality are then a priori excluded from the experience of the average person.

Society not only "orders" the experience of its members by means of its language (which is always the concrete echo of a particular mentality or spirit); what is more, it filters these experiences by means of a number of social taboos. In other words, society places a "filter" before our eyes, which "does not allow certain feelings to reach consciousness and which is inclined to expel them from that area as soon as they might reach it."[1] A filter is an instrument whose purpose is purification. It works by letting light rays of only one specific color pass through it while it excludes others.

The question in our day is: Which experiences should be excluded or repressed because they are improper, dangerous, or "medieval," and therefore should be relegated to the unconscious, and which ones should have access to our conscious awareness? We can exclude the harmful rays. But we can also keep rays necessary to life from being seen. Most of the time now experiences which do not correspond with the "outlook" or the current universe of ideas of the group to which the individual belongs get repressed. "Repression" is a Freudian concept. It concerns a form of inner defensiveness and rejection of experiences which could lead to tensions with the society in which one lives. For that reason, "disturbing" experiences get diverted toward the forgotten crannies of the unconscious. The good of the group is considered more important than the unfolding of individual personality.

Whatever may or may not be consciously experienced varies according to the culture in which one lives. A Papuan does not need to repress as much as a New York banker. The life of a Papuan is much simpler and less complicated. The acceptability of experiences also varies according to the historical period in which one is born. The Victorian Puritan regarded "life" differently from the way the modern student views it.

It is to the credit of J. H. Van den Berg that he was the first to have expressly pointed out the historicity or "metabletica" of the human world of experience, and, consequently, of whatever is unconscious or not experienced. The contents of the unconscious are indeed subject to change. The unconscious is an historically evolving reservoir into which is dumped whatever a given society looks on as immoral or superfluous and hence refuses to *see* any longer. It would be well worth the effort to take a look at the reservoir of modern collective unconscious, and especially to compare its contents with what was repressed in the time of Freud who, shortly before the century's end, first called attention to the existence of the unconscious.

In bourgeois Victorian culture, sexual experiences as a rule were disposed of as improper, unacceptable, and even perverse. The consequences of this are only now coming to light. "Chase away nature and it comes back at a gallop," goes an old French saying. The proportions that eroticism is now taking on in literature, film, advertising, recreation, etc., are so great that they scarcely leave room for other human experiences. Just as Freud would have it, only the formerly taboo explanation of sexuality is considered as the source of every neurosis. Consequently the modern who is clearly liberated as far as that sphere is concerned must be a model of *joie de vivre* and of satisfactory psychic balance. In reality, however, more people, especially the young, appear to be dissatisfied, frustrated and disappointed than ever before. "Something else" is wrong, apparently. That "something else" which people are missing in our days Laing calls "the internal world." Van den Berg speaks of "spirituality." What remains on the conscious level is the ordinary, banal and material world of everyday, without much thinking, without much idealism, without much of an idea of life and death. It is a secularized world of mediocrity never penetrated by any genuine form of transcendence.

"The most striking illustration (of the loss of spirituality) is given by the modern cloister, which, as everyone knows, is rapidly getting empty. Contemplation, meditation, abnegation, mysticism, which all told mean being consciously in the sector of spirituality, are apparently coming to an end."[2] No essential human need can be made or kept unconscious definitively and neither can the religious need. Since Western civilization has awakened sexually, we cannot also keep it sleeping religiously for ever.

For the present, however, the average person no longer has the necessary spiritual senses or experience channels for the religious dimension. It certainly *seems* that God is dead. Why? Because our spiritual faculties for eventually encountering God are somehow out of order. The social "filter" placed before our eyes "protects" us from disturbing religious light. Since the "Enlightenment," we have come to be, surprisingly enough, in an increasingly greater religious darkness.

Viktor Frankl, the modern successor of Freud in his chair of psychiatry and neurology at the University of Vienna, says: "Our time is no longer like Freud's, a time of sexual frustration. We are experiencing an existential frustration. It is youth, above all, who feel frustrated in their search for the meaning of life. . . . The patients who turn to us today suffer, in fact, ever more clearly from the feeling of inward emptiness, a feeling of the total absence of any meaning for their existence."[3] According to Frankl, psychiatrists have nothing to say to believers who find security in the Mystery to which they are bound. But the great problem is the non-religious person who turns to the psychiatrist out of yearning for an answer to the most fundamental questions of life. When the priest no longer has the needed answers, then people make psychiatrists into "medical priests" and "secularized confessors."[4]

How can we explain it if individuals in certain circumstances show an inclination, contrary to nature, to repress personal experiences, or at least to allow their field of experience to be shriveled up by the filter which the social milieu places before their eyes? First of all, there is an urge for a certain spiritual coziness, a dread of standing alone with our personal outlook on things. We need to know that we are safely surrounded by people who "see" things as we see them, namely, who see things just as little as we do. We want at all cost to avoid standing alone, or to be labeled as "naive" or "passé." We associate ourselves with the view of the group, even though this supposes an abdication from our own experiences.

In the wake of Max Scheler, sociologists of knowledge have pointed out how the milieu in which I live "rules" or governs my thinking. Social psychologists like Musafer Sherif have proved this same thing experimentally at Harvard with regard to sense perception. My perceptions are influenced by those in my immediate physical proximity who "perceive" or do not "perceive" the same thing. If my neighbors estimate the distance between two separate lights as only five inches, and I myself originally judged it to be one yard, then I feel that I am practically obliged to lower my estimate substantially. The cause? It is always dread of being the only one "out of tune." Scheler particularly researched the manner in which a group comes to the same "insight." He established that personal experiences suppose a "framework of thought" or a "cognitive system." Society imperceptibly bestows this system on its members and implants it in them so that they can organize, understand, and "place" their own subjective experiences.

There are simplistic as well as richly-differentiated cognitive systems. The degree of differentiation determines the finesse of the nuances of which our powers of perception are capable. The cruder and less developed our spiritual framework the poorer our experiences. By "cognitive system" Scheler has more in mind than a mere receiving and ordering station for our experiences. A Harvard scholar utilizes a more complex thought system than does a Papuan. A child thinks more simply than an adult. Geniuses and artists respectively often break out of current thought patterns and structures of experience. Nevertheless, even a genius has had masters, and an artist such as Manet is unthinkable apart from the impressionistic school of Paris.

Dread of a possibly skeptical smile with which my milieu might receive the account of my personal experiences diminishes when I hear the reassuring applause of everyone around me. If these people look surprised, shocked, or amused, then the question arises immediately within me: "Perhaps I am making a fool of myself? Maybe my experience was an illusion?"

Fear of being regarded as old-fashioned or passé makes a person gradually change his or her outlook on life. Consequently, such an individual interprets personal experiences differently, in the light of what is considered to be a more adapted, modern and successful mentality. As Peter Berger has noted, "Only the madman or the rare case of genius can inhabit a world of meaning all by himself. Most of us acquire our meanings from other men and require their constant support, so that these meanings may continue to be believable."[5] For Christians that is the meaning of Church formation. There we find people who think as we do, and, above all, who experience God as we do; hence, they support and strengthen us in our belief. A hippie, too, needs a milieu or sub-culture of fellow-hippies in order to keep the chosen life style meaningful and livable.

Changing our concept of life involves, as far as our social relationships are concerned, entering along new pathways. We willingly surround ourselves with those who think as we do. Someone who becomes a worker-priest will soon be more conversant with dockworkers than with seminary professors. The inverse is also true. A new circle of friends and a new social milieu will inevitably change, either infecting or fructifying, our world of experience. The farmer's son who goes to the university in order to study positive sciences will sooner or later become a "foreigner" in the eyes of his earlier agricultural community. This is why so many choose safe coziness over the adventure of new discovery. Dread is still the great enemy of personal experience.

A second reason for the denial or restriction of personal experience is of a moral order. Personal decisions or position-taking not supported by the group costs more energy than submissive, passive doing-as-others-do.

Had the citizens of the Bavarian town of Dachau "known," had it penetrated their consciousness, that the foul smell which two strange factory chimneys were spreading over their roofs was caused by the macabre cremation of the corpses of hundreds of thousands of gassed Jews, they would have been morally obliged to take a stand against it. A moral protest, however, could have cost their lives. Therefore, countless citizens did not "know" what happened there in the camp. They had no idea what had been done to the Jews: they did not "believe" what the BBC reported about it. If they had become aware of it, they would have been obliged to make a terribly dangerous decision. But what can one do against the superior power of an immoral enemy? Better to imagine that it is not all *that* serious!

The same was true concerning child labor in the mines during the nineteenth century. Only those who neither knew nor saw it could enjoy a comfortable ease of conscience. Did these know-nothings, therefore, have no guilt? On the contrary, their great guilt lay precisely in the fact that they did not see (they did not want to, did not dare to, and, therefore, *could* not see) what they should have seen. The admonition of Christ addressed to the only class of people with whom he seemed particularly severe, the Pharisees, had to do with their "poverty of experience" or culpable blindness. "Their ears are heavy of hearing and their eyes they have closed, lest they should perceive with their eyes, and hear with their ears, and understand with their heart" (Mt 13:15).

What moral guilt did the Pharisees have who ultimately did away with Christ? Did they intend to murder the Son of God? They were neither so stupid nor so naive. In their eyes, they had done nothing more than act *in good faith* to get rid of a menace, a sacrilegious agitator. They did not know any better and meant well. However, they were guilty because, after the Lord's countless signs and his impressive words, they still had not *seen* that this man could not be an ordinary man but that he was the Messiah.

Experiencing or not experiencing is at root a moral question; indeed, it is the very core of human morality—hence its great importance. Every person has the duty to be open to reality and to inquire into it. The argument, "I did not know it; if I knew it, I would have acted otherwise," is worthless in most cases. It is precisely this "not knowing" and this "not having seen" which constitute a person's guilt when there is question of guilt.

"Then they (the sinners) also will answer: Lord, when did we see thee hungry or thirsty, or a stranger or naked or sick or in prison?" (Mt 25:44). They will be reproached for the fact that, in spite of the Lord's admonition, they have not recognized the deeper essence of the poor; they have not "seen" that behind the face of the needy the Lord himself was concealed.

"Stupidity is a more dangerous enemy of the good than malice," according to Bonhoeffer. "It is a moral rather than an intellectual defect.... (The stupid man) is under a spell, he is blinded; ... a passive instrument, he will be capable of any evil and at the same time incapable of seeing that it is evil."[6] Immorality is a question of conscience, of knowing (con-science) or of not knowing and not seeing what we could and should have seen. The immoral man or woman does not "see" or "grasp" at all the injury or harm being done to fellow human beings. He or she, "seeing" only the immediate self, is "tactless" and "short-sighted"—hence, experience-poor.

Finally, it is not only the anxious and ignorant individual who frequently limits or falsifies personal experience; various social groups consciously meddle with the experiential world of their members. Each group (church, state, party, order, etc.) is inclined to harbor suspicion against all the free and original thinkers in its ranks. Full-grown adults, who proceed on their own experiences and insights and act conscientiously, as a rule are regarded as disturbing and confusing influences for the totalitarian form of groups. The French sociologist E. Durkheim sees society as "a moral order," a group of individuals who respect certain norms and rules of behavior. He calls the principle upon which such a moral order is based "a disciplined mentality." There is no possible doubt that without order and coherence a society has no chance of survival. Yet "disciplined mentality" is an ambiguous concept. The inhuman and immoral side of social life can be remedied only when exceptional and privileged minds are allowed the possibility of raising their voices to show the way. A group which intends not only to preserve what has already been gained but also to improve what is not yet satisfactory should have access to the creativity of some of its members. Persons with a genuine founder's or reformer's vocation, however, are not numerous, not even in the Church. Bergson says: "Look at it how you will, you must always come back to the conception of moral creators who see in their mind's eye a new social atmosphere, an environment in which life would be more worth living, I mean a society such that, if men once tried it, they would refuse to go back to the old state of things. Thus only is moral progress to be defined. . . ."[7]

No historical renewal or reform is ever born from the spontaneous activity of the masses. The creative moment was always the free play of a mind endowed with genius, of a personality with a new, corrected outlook on the old reality. If Solzhenitsyn can no longer be content with the existing Soviet society, then that society has two options. Either it listens to his voice and allows his prophetic word to reveal the course of the social evolution, or else it begins to speak of him as "a danger for the people" and of a "subversive, undisciplined mentality." But a culture which silences, exiles, or bans its most vital minds is doomed to stagnation in the morass of a lifeless "status quo" if not ultimately to actual destruction.

If culture, in fact, is a question of "ordering of experience," then the central question is: "*Who* is it who orders that experience here, and who is it who opens up new perspectives or points of view here? Is it the great creative minds, or is it the established bureaucreatic institutions? Is it creative persons or preservation minded institutions? Seen in this way, the dilemma is demagogical and useless. Within each culture, human experience is ordered through institutions which in turn continually grow out of the thinking of creative minds (even though these institutions later often grow askew or in time get moth-eaten). No great creative mind ever hindered the *élan vital* from operating in later generations, too. The greatest founders and reformers even hoped that this would be the case, and therefore they constantly left room for freedom of experience and thinking among their disciples. By no means does this mean that a genuine *personal* experience, which religious experience always is, could only fall to the lot of geniuses, rebels, or revolutionaries. Rather, it means that each society or group which wants to be viable and to remain so must be socially ordered and must be able to reckon on the loyalty of its members. Such an ordering is necessary for the simple conduct of business and for facilitating human relations.

On the other hand, though, if the same society does not want to become atrophied and turn into a ghetto, it must leave room for the creativity of those of its members who are able to make a significant contribution. In particular this is true for reli-

gious societies—churches or sects. The social order, as it lies before us, is neither the only one possible nor the best one
imaginable. It is subject to review and further humanizing, as
history can certainly teach us. Whether renewal happens in a
revolutionary manner or comes about gradually, it is always the
result of "insight" from people who, on the one hand, make no
unconditional peace with the existing situation, but, on the other hand, know a satisfying interior peace so that they do not go
off the track into brusk or chaotic improvisation. These are people who rise out of the warm coziness of the familiar and develop an "eye" for something that their colleagues have neither
noticed nor yet encountered. The alert eye of such "pilots" discovers a new light on the horizon, or receives a hitherto unnoticed signal that could ultimately bring the whole crew to change
the ship's course. Whoever would do away with these pilots
withdraws any chance of discovery from the society or group.

A time such as ours, in which the experience of the average
person seems to be seriously one-sided and shriveled, needs
more than ever those who see more than what people have been
taught to regard as "normal" and who are aware of more than
the silent majority experiences. We will need to consult these individuals if we wish to be roused from the spiritual hibernation
in which the monotony of technical materialism has steadily im-
mersed us. But will the safe cave-dwellers be sufficiently open to
believe in these alert witnesses of the living Light? That is the
question which becomes increasingly acute in every time of crisis.

• 3 •

Enrichment of Experience

Because of the richness of their personal experience, some people possess the ability to shake others out of their spiritual lethargy and to point out the blind spots in their faculties of perception. "Great souls have the property of being able to discover the principal need of the times in which they live and to consecrate themselves to it," wrote Lacordaire. To know precisely what is lacking in the mentality of the times, namely, what is repressed or forgotten, has always distinguished great from ordinary people. The great continually bear witness to dimensions lost to view. Artists seem especially apt for this task of warning us. Certain "charismatic" personalties have always been extremely important wherever the deeper meaning of human experiences is concerned. We use the term "charismatics" in the sense which Max Weber gave this word: religiously-inspired, exceptionally-talented personalities, who, driven by a renewed vision of things, knew how to alter, abolish, or to fundamentally renew existing traditions, and who were usually immediately followed in this task by a crowd of enthusastic disciples. Think of striking personalities such as Buddha, Socrates, Ignatius, Luther, or, in our times, Roger Schutz.

Where the experience of God is more particularly concerned, in addition to artists and charismatic founders we have the mystics. Insofar as their gifts do not overlap, artists, charismatics and mystics are those who through their word or unique manner of seeing are able to open up the *horizon of experiences* for their disciples. There is no other path to enrichment of experience than an encounter, in person or through reading, with such a great personality.

Artists have always issued warnings about the flaws and one-sidedness of the culture in which they lived. In the bourgeois nineteenth century, sexuality was more and more undernourished, so that it finally disappeared almost altogether from human awareness. Flaubert saw through this. Forty years previous to Freud's first scientific publication about the sexual drive, Flaubert had already written his *Madame Bovary.* The erotic atrophy into which men wanted to relegate women would lead to disastrous consequences. But his message would not be understood. Both the ecclesiastical Index and bourgeois criticism were in opposition to Flaubert. As a result, sexuality would go on being invisible until nature itself would take bold revenge.

Even to our own day, erotic literature has been overflowing the dikes of the old proprieties in a very tempestuous way. Meanwhile, the religious dimension sank, unnoticed, into the unconscious. The reality of the supernatural would not be completely silenced. In fact, religion no longer speaks to modern man. The average person today has a little "feeling" for it as the puritanical Anna O. had for eroticism. Once again, the greatest artists have complained of this modern forgetfulness. Their voice, it is true, is not silenced by an Index or reprisals. They are simply no longer understood. "What? Solzhenitsyn—a warning witness for us about the religious dimension of life? Isn't he just heckling the Soviet government?" Many "see" nothing more than that in him. "Saint-John Perse—a poet about Transcendence?" Most "see" in his writings no more than hermetical, musical, symbolic splendor. The voice of these great writers, in fact, is neither that of a propagandist for the sake of good, nor that of a recruiting zealot. Rather, it is a discreetly suggesting voice which betrays a finely tuned instrument of inner experience. "Let him who has understanding understand . . ." is what it seems the artist is whispering to us. It is no surprise that great artists are seldom understood in their own time. Their words of witness are consciously shrouded in the same veil of discretion with which a happily married woman conceals her most intimate experiences. Serious people do not toss personal experiences of happiness out for grabs to the public. Nevertheless, the artist cannot keep silent: "For out of the abundance of the heart, the mouth speaks" (Mt 12:34). At the same time, the artist is afraid to prostitute that which belongs most intimately to the life of the soul. Things totally transcending everyday affairs are described using the suggestive power of symbolism. Only those who could ever experience something analogous can understand. More than lucid intellect is needed if one would deeply feel a love poem. Someone who has never loved is incapable of understanding love poetry. Nevertheless, even the most rigid Puritan claims to know what a love poem is all about, perhaps seeing in it teenage emotions which will disappear quickly, like mist, under the sun of maturity. Likewise, the most rabid atheist claims to understand exactly what is meant by "religious experience": namely, illusory projections which will gradually be dissolved by scientific "enlightenment."

No religiously-inspired person cashes in on such experiences. We can confidently take it as axiomatic that anyone who parades those religious experiences, even if it be with "edifying" intentions, suffers from self-deception. No mystic ever published his or her experiences "in order to do good." Thérèse of Lisieux, as was the case with so many others like her, was obliged by her superior to write down her spiritual history so it could be checked. It became the well-known *Story of a Soul.* The

poor girl had never imagined that her writings would get printed and spread. It was not her humility that opposed such a
thing, but rather her lucid understanding that no real lover ever
makes public the intimacies of a personal love relationship.

Hence, it would appear that the artist is always ahead of the
times. Strictly speaking, this is not the case. On the contrary, the
artist is the only one who fully experiences the present with
open eyes, who has a notion of its greatest positive qualities and
its most gaping lacunae. In other words, the artist recognizes the
"signs of the times" and can write an account of the future coming upon us precisely because he or she is so conscious of what
is now going on. Artists will discuss openly that which most are
keeping silent about and name aloud what most have forgotten.
"We sing only of absent things," wrote the poet Valéry. That
D. H. Lawrence had, posthumously, such an enormous success
with his *Lady Chatterley's Lover* (the book in his lifetime was strictly forbidden; the sleeping dog of eroticism was not supposed to
be awakened) only shows that the danger to which Lawrence
wanted to allude was already alive.

While hundreds of little second generation Flauberts or
Lawrences in our day are still boring us with erotic literature
which has become superfluous, great literature has for a long
time already turned toward new horizons. Now that sexuality
has taken on enormous proportions, religious experience has
become a rare bird, a "species" which appears to have almost
died out in popular literature. And yet people need not be exceptionally gifted to see how many genuine artists discreetly but
persistently warn against the new spiritual mutilation that has
been done to modern men and women, the amputation of their
ties with God which have made their faith unconscious. Almost
the entire series of post-war Nobel Prize winners in literature
deal, directly or indirectly, with the problem of "God become
unconscious."

How do artists help their contemporaries see what really is

there to be observed by open eyes? How do they succeed in pointing out forgotten dimensions to others? An example may clarify this. For ages, Switzerland was regarded as an ugly, inhospitable and bare region. However, J. J. Rousseau, seized by the grandiose austerity of the Alpine scenery, was able, by his works, to make Europe aware of this sort of hidden beauty. A hundred years later, it was considered to be in good taste to find snowy mountains, waterfalls, and rocks "beautiful." In this way, the artist Rousseau taught people to see something which was certainly there before, but which at the time was scarcely noticed by anyone.

We have to be grateful to painters such as Cézanne and Van Gogh if we see in the Provencal Mount St. Victoire more than an arid, chalky desert. Yet, it was not the intention of Van Gogh and Cézanne to fire us up for more tourism in Provence. Rather, they simply painted what they "saw," but they painted it so poignantly that others also began to "see" it. Modern spiritually charged masters of literature are likewise not trying to recruit (or to recapture) new members for emptied-out church buildings. No great artist is ever a zealot for a church or for a sect. Rather, these artists feel themselves driven to speak out what they have experienced interiorly or what has struck them with astonishment. Through their intervention others are brought to look in the same direction, and to a gradual awareness of rediscovery of something new. Meanwhile, Van Gogh and Cézanne died poor and, for the most part, misunderstood. If today's witnesses of the "God-become-unconscious" phenomenon are not yet dead, and if some of them even receive a Nobel Prize, the question still remains as to how many really understand what they are pointing to and suggesting.

By way of illustration, let us examine how one of these great men describes the task of the poet. Saint-John Perse was an intimate friend of the converts and poets T. S. Eliot, Paul Claudel, and W. H. Auden, as well as of the Swedish mystic Dag Hammarskjöld. What bound these friends together is clear only for those who, without bias, read their works and their mutual correspondence. Each of them draws from the same source, a source which today lies quite overgrown with the thick abundant weeds of pure externality. In Perse's book *Winds* (*Vents*) (the invisible but powerful wind is a symbol of God) we read: "And the poet, too, is with us, on the pathway of the men of his times. . . . His business among us: clarification of messages. And the reply given in him by illumination of the heart. Not the writings but the thing itself. Taken in its essence and in its entirety. Conservation not of copies but of originals. And the poet's writing follows the hearing. . . . Man infected with dreams, man overcome by the divine infection. Not one of those seeking stupor in the vapors of hashish, like Scythians. . . . But careful for his lucidity, jealous of his authority, and holding up to the wind the full noontime of his vision: The cry! The god's piercing cry! may it seize you in the midst of the crowd, not in your chambers. And broadcast by the crowd may it reverberate in even to the limits of perception!"[1]

If we substitute, in the first sentence, the word "priest" for "poet," we find here an exact description of the most urgent priestly task. Our age needs priests who are guides, ready to lead people seeking their way back into the lost land of the interior life. And who but the one who knows the mountains from his own experience is a fit guide in the Alps? As an artist is for Saint-John Perse, so also is the priest a spiritual leader above all. Far from inciting people to safe flight from the world where they can be content with the pleasures of their little, walled-up, private spiritual lives, the priest must march with the people along their streets ("on the pathway of the men of his times"). Consciously bearing good news, the priestly vocation is to make this message intelligible and to interpret it, preferably from interior enlightenment and personal experience ("by illumination of the heart") and not from theories or bookish wisdom ("not writings, but the thing itself") The priest is not a theological theorist but a person who is spiritually alive.

The difference between Pasolini's film *The Gospel According to St. Matthew* and Matthew's Gospel itself lies in the fact that Pasolini looks at only one aspect, that of the social-justice Jesus who pits himself against the powerful Pharisees, while the evangelist offers an eye-witness account with a sense of the whole. In contrast to Pasolini, Matthew does not bring us a partial message which might seem to accord with modern tastes for the time being. He sees an integral whole, including those aspects which are less popular at any given time. Is the task of a doctor meekly to prescribe for a patient's self-diagnosed needs? Is it not rather the physician's duty to explain to the patient (who comes seeking advice out of ignorance of the cause of the malady) exactly what is wrong?

The artist never plagiarizes a general theory. An artistic expression is always the immediate result ("the bearing") of a unique personal experience. Others may further generalize or systematize; the artist deals with the authentic original.

For Saint-John Perse, the poet is one who is "touched" (in the etymological meaning of the word) by the divinity. He cannot wrench himself free of its grip. He seems quite possessed by it. He does not build up for himself an artificially-expanded world of experience, using exotic drugs ("not one of those seeking stupor . . . like Scythians"). The experience of God simply overcomes him.

Far from exposing his uncertainties in the framework of false modesty, the lucid poet *knows* that he who has "seen" something with his own eyes is also rendered fit for sharing what he saw with others ("careful for his lucidity, jealous of his authority"). For that reason he does not jump on the bandwagon of the stylish spirituality of groping and seeking. The cult of uncertainty and doubt and the jargon of vagueness are foreign to him. He knows, for he has seen. He speaks forth what he has experienced.

The language of a real priest, as also the word of an inspired poet, is the result of God's speaking within ("God's piercing cry"). In order to hear God's word in us, it is similarly necessary to push our powers of experiencing "to the limits of perception." And so we have to look farther than the length of the average person's nose.

Those whom Weber calls "the charismatics" form a second group of people who seem to us to be able to give us an eye for the unseen and unheard. These persons never draw their astonishing authority from themselves. They know that they are "sent" and are acting under mandate from a higher authority; whether they call it a "Daemon" as does Socrates, or "the Lord Jesus" as Ignatius prefers, remains for the time being outside our scope. Their edifying influence, or as some would prefer to say "their constructive thinking," consists in a new look at life and in a new life-style which flows from it. All of this comes from the fascinating power of attraction emanating from them, spontaneously and unwilled among the genuine charismatics, calculated and contrived and consciously sought after among false charismatics, i.e., among demagogues and zealots. For Bergson, genuine religious personalities are "exceptional people with crowds in their train. They ask nothing and yet they obtain. They have no need to exhort; they have only to exist; their very existence is a call."[2]

Max Weber was the first who has described sociologically the important role of the charismatic within each organized religion. For him, charisma is the counterpart of existing religious institutions, of ecclesiastical routine, of clerical office, and of traditional formality. Weber views the history of each religion as a continuous alternation between revolutionary founders or reformers (charismatics) on the one side and inevitable resulting routines (Veralltäglichung) maintained through institutions, rules, orders and laws on the other side. In other words, each *de facto* religious institution always has a history behind it, out of which it grew and from which it is the ultimate result. The principal actor or founder of this history was always a "charismatic."

Take the charismatics away from religion, that is, kill the prophets or make speaking and life impossible for them, and religion will splinter and disintegrate. On the other hand, if a religious group or church, sighing for "charismatic movement," rejects rational structure and stable order, then in the long run this group will degenerate into an untenable formlessness or chaos. History demonstrates again and again that a situation of constant and intense excitement has an undermining effect on spiritual life. By definition, life is found only in an "organism." "Stable institutions are the measuring rod of a people's capabilities. To live outside of them means alienation for a person,"[3] says Gehlen. The charismatic who acts from vocation, not from psychological excitement, is the only one who performs genuinely creative work as far as institutions are concerned, even though this creation of new forms may lie outside the charismatic's conscious intention. Standing "outside the ordinary," charismatic figures become the cause of disciples going out to stand in their footsteps in order to see what they saw and experience what they experienced. When several disciples find themselves standing on the same path, then there follows a new institution.

This is why charismatics are the real "movers" of religious renewal. In spite of themselves, they are the creators of different life-styles. They are models in the sense that the originality of the charismatic becomes the "image" after which many want to fashion themselves or, at least, from whom many receive inspiration. To repeat: they neither directly intend this nor have it in mind. "They ask nothing." The charismatic is not an organizer, manager or politician even though his or her disciples may continually ask for that. They just live. Yet, "models attract us."

Next to the well-trod and fixed paths of existing tradition, charismatics blaze new trails through the forest of possibilities, paths along which others will follow. They do not merely wriggle through the underbrush of life. Rather, they chop out a pathway, their footsteps becoming a new "way of life."

Nevertheless, charismatics do not intend to offer any "safe foothold" for those lacking inspiration. They do not want to be figures others can model themselves after, or under whose responsibility the timid can find shelter for their lack of conscience. They do not set up their own persons as central; they seek no clinging adherents or worshipers. Rather, they direct their disciples toward the "wholly Other." This is why we cannot call Christ a charismatic figure. The charismatic is a channel flowing and leading to God. But Christ, on the contrary, is the point of arrival, the cornerstone, the "omega point." For Mohammed, only Allah counted. John the Baptist callled himself the precursor and friend of the Bridegroom. But Christ calls himself "the truth" and "the life." Christianity cannot be reduced to an ideally human following of the self-annihilating Jesus. Being a Christian means encountering the living and present person of Christ in a permanent manner.

In *The Brothers Karamazov,* Dostoevsky depicts not only the well-institutionalized monastery but also the "charismatic" staretz Zossima. It is Zossima, not the monks, who attracts young and old. His authentic experience of God becomes a source of inspiration for all of the religious life around him. His task is giving others "insight" into the Scriptures. Yet he is not speaking in his own self-assured name; he knows that he is simply one who is sent. He is a sign, a guidepost, on the way to God. People do not cling to guideposts; they go by them. They do not, however, forget them.

In our times, have not Roger Schutz, Martin Luther King Jr., Helder Camara, Thomas Merton, Carol Carretto and Ivan Illich lived out for us many new "ways of being Christian"? Religious life is indeed pluriform: the various spiritualities or Christian life-styles now existing all bear the proper charismatic stamp of their respective founders. Charismatics are "edifying" insofar as their manner of existing opens up new perspectives for others.

Weber recognized that the great problem of charisma is the difficulty of establishing the routine which inevitably follows the short-lived intensity of every formation period. The group of the apostles was succeeded by a hierarchical Church structure. Stable, rational dogmas developed out of the direct words they received from the Lord. Ignatius' personal experiences grew into an "order" with well-defined "constitutions," and from what happened in Taizé, a "Rule of Taizé" was eventually distilled. Ignatius knew that a rule could no more lead to an experience of God than strict marriage morality could ever lead to love; in both cases, the cart follows the horse. Nevertheless, he was obliged by his followers to write down how he saw the life of a Jesuit. Why, in spite of everything, did he accede to their request? On the one hand, he knew that no new structure would ever be apt for leading to a new experience of God or for religious renewal. On the other hand, he also saw clearly that the inverse was true: namely, that religious renewal necessarily seeks new forms if it is to be more than an enthusiastic flash-in-the-pan. No one wants to live without structure or without form. It is the vocation of the human person, created according to the image of the Creator, to give "form" in a creative way, to the wild chaos of the many possibilities open to us.

After a span of time, religious forms, which are always the hardened product of charismatic life, get too far removed from the original experience. They then appear faded, hollow, anachronistic or passé. That is when people complain of formalism (i.e., form without content) or doctrines unrelated to life. As a consequence, the believer feels nostalgia for a more authentic, a more thoroughly felt, and more intensely lived religious experi-

ence. From this perspective, charismatic movements are typical.
They crop up chronically in the life of the Church. They always
betray a striking hunger for experience and an allergy to organization and functionality.

What is important for them is not who *de facto* received the
office of priest from the Church, but rather who *now* feels moved
by the Spirit? The accent is on the new, the spontaneous, the im-
provisatory and the immediate. Mediation by religious function-
aries or priests appears superfluous. Rubrics, sacramental rites
or ecclesiastical law they call juridicism. Formality is labeled
"formalism." Better an incomprehensible cry "straight from the
heart" than an ancient religious formula. The hunger for new
life can become so intense that they can forget that culture is essentially an "ordering of experience." Charismatic movements
always come into being in times of crisis or transition, times
hankering after *new* forms. No form was ever brought into being
by a formless group. Creation is always the work of an inspired
personality. It was personalities like this that Weber identified as
"charismatic."

The successful rise of Protestantism and the various forms
of the resulting sects were typical of this impulse for "revival."
Formalistic, bureaucratic and dogmatic Church structures all
too removed from the original biblical community were particularly "protested" against. The protest took form, and thereby
gained a chance of succeeding, in charismatically moved persons
such as Luther and Calvin. The intensity of their writings and
the genuineness of their personal experience of God appealed
to thousands. Confronted by the Lutheran Church which followed upon Luther, pietistic and pentecostal sects have continually attempted to stir up the embers of religious immediacy.
And it could be argued that the charismatic personality of John
XXIII alone caused more movement in the Catholic Church
than the whole collection of theological documents composed
under his leadership by hundreds of council fathers and their

advisors. But the charismatic who would hinder or disdain form giving dooms his or her work to speedy and inevitable chaos and demise. Forms and structures are the only soil in which living experience can take root in a lasting way.

Sooner or later every charismatic is confronted with the problem of the second generation. Naturally, a growing number of disciples means leadership, organization, and even real bureaucracy. The place of the charismatic is soon taken by an expertly schooled disciple who shows more talent for organization than authentic inspiration. Weber saw the prototype of this progression from charisma to function realized in the Catholic Church. Here it is no longer a prophet kindled with enthusiasm but an efficient leader-figure who is sought after. This is how the inspiring reformer John of the Cross was expelled before he died from his own order, specifically by the second generation. Relieved from all exercise of authority, he was obliged to withdraw into the solitude of a hermitage. His successor was the Italian Doria, "a powerful man with talent, skill, and ability—a cool, decisive, narrow and despotic organizer." "From John of the Cross to Doria, we have the brusk passage from mystical dream to impure mixture of the political and religious levels. . . . Is it only a coincidence if Doria's innovations introduced into the reformed Carmel administrative fragmentation and oligarchic tyranny?"[4]

In a post-charismatic, "factual" time, the main concern comes to be competency and human talent. The important thing now is the "function" or "office" in which one is placed via the juridical ecclesiastical procedures. The question is always whether someone is endowed with sufficient gifts of "management" in order to lead a group efficiently.

Throughout the entire history of the Church there have been periods of charismatic revival (new orders arise, saints make a deep impression on believers, etc.) followed by periods of stabilization and government. On the heels of the troubled times of the Reformation, of Ignatius and also of Teresa of Avila, there followed a restructuring through the Council of Trent on the one hand, and the establishment of Lutheran, Reformed, and Anglican Churches on the other. It is easy to understand that the hunger for charismatic renewal usually cropped up in periods during which it was felt that the bureaucratic establishment was all too crass.

In what, concretely, does the enriching influence of a charismatic upon his disciples' world of experience consist? Persons such as Helder Camara and Martin Luther King, modern day "prophets" rather than skillful administrators, "saw" situations crying to heaven for vengeance but which had gone unnoticed for years. What they saw, they also spoke about, in accordance with the word of Peter and John: "We cannot but speak of what we have seen and heard" (Acts 4:20). Because of their word of witness, more and more people began to "see" what is going on in North and South America. They also made it much easier to "see" clearly what is going on elsewhere.

In a less spectacular way, the charismatic also can be helpful to believers of all times by giving them an "eye" for what can go on in their own souls. To be sure, the charismatic arouses no visions in his or her disciples. There can be, however, an awakening in the consciousness of an unbiased reader or disciple. In a letter to a friend, the religious psychologist William James bemoaned his own religious emptiness. Nevertheless, he said, the many religious visionaries whom he had studied had been a precious help to him: "I have no living sense of commerce with God. Though I am so devoid of direct awareness of God in the strongest sense of the word, yet there is something in me which makes response when I hear utterances made from that league. I hear a deeper voice within me. Something tells me, thither lies truth."[5]

In the foreword of his book *Celebration of Awareness,* Illich writes: "Institutions create certainties, and, taken seriously, certainties deaden the heart and shackle the imagination."[6]

The charismatic, who by definition is the opposite of the established institution, continually produces the inverse effect, an effect which may be necessary in a time of religious stagnation or underdevelopment. The charismatic points to the insufficiency of the tried and true, not by calming our hearts but rather by enkindling them. Nothing stirs our imagination so powerfully as the inspiring word of the gifted charismatic.

Some charismatics have also been mystics. The mystics form a third group of persons who appear to enrich experience. Grandmaison describes their significance for the average believer as follows: "The great mystics are the pioneers and the heroes of the most beautiful, the most desirable, and the most marvelous of worlds. Hearing them, our souls tremble with hope and expectation. . . . The experiences of these forerunners are like documents entrusted to us, brought back by explorers of almost inaccessible lands."[7]

The mystics speak to us about a reality which often appears to the average believer as exotic and far-flung, if not totally unreal. But the reality, in fact, lies much closer to us than the average believer suspects. The mystic experiences fully what the ordinary believer only accepts as true and believes. The difference is of a phenomenological sort. The same God is experienced by the mystic and by the ordinary believer, respectively, in different degrees of intensity. The mystic very consciously experiences the relationship between the human person and God. For the ordinary believer, however, this relationship with God is a reality to which credence is given, but which is not experienced in the same degree of overwhelming clarity and evidence. We find testimonials of mystics in all great religions. They are always phenomenological descriptions of what it is to meet God. Hence, the mystic experiences psychologically what the theologian describes conceptually and rationally. Mysticism is concerned with experience; theology is concerned with theory.

Is it possible to describe with any exactitude just what constitutes the mystical experience? The term "mysticism" is used
and misused with the most diverse meanings. For some, it
means an irrational ideology—for example, the "mysticism of
Nazism." For others, mysticism is rather a mysterious, emotional manner of knowing, upon which sober science has no grip: in
other words, a phenomenon belonging to parapsychology. Yet
others hold mysticism to be an experience of extraordinary phenomena, such as visions, prophecies, stigmata, bilocation, etc.
Nevertheless, all great mystics warn against the totally accidental, peripheral, and altogether non-essential character of such
occasional phenomena.

First and foremost, mysticism is sentient knowledge and experience of God or, as Gerson calls it, a "cognitio experimenta-
lis; experimental knowledge." It is, therefore, direct knowledge,
a living experience of God gained neither as a result of ascetical
effort nor as a reward for a morally irreproachable life but given
as a totally unmerited gift to a few chosen persons. It comes
over these persons entirely unexpectedly and without any no-
ticeable psychological preparation or cause. As the fourteenth
century Flemish mystic Ruusbroec has described it, "No one can
arrive at this through his own skill or through any subtlety, or
through any effort whatsoever. Only those whom God wants to
unite with himself in their spirit and to enlighten with his own
light are empowered to contemplate God, but it is given to no
one else. . . . And, therefore, he gives light when he wills, where
he wills, and to whom he wills, and to the degree he wills."[8]

To affirm that mystics remain "passive" certainly does not
mean that they do nothing. On the contrary, mystics tend to be
particularly active, but their activity does not flow out of their
own egos. The source of their activity is no longer personal initiative but God himself who stands at the helm of their initiative.
Therefore, the mystic can say joyfully, with Saint-John Perse:
"You weigh upon my heart and govern my members, O my love,

like the Master of the vessel. Sweet the bar under the Master's pressure. . . ."

While the mystic is moved by God, he or she painfully experiences a sense of inadequacy in putting that experience of God into words understandable to the rest of society. "While I speak about these things, I reproach myself as I go over these words and expressions. They are inexact compared with what I feel—without any feeling—and with what resists being grasped,"[9] according to Catherine of Genoa (1447–1510). So it is no accident that the greatest of the mystics known to us also appear to be virtuosos of language, or even poets, at the same time. We have only to think of the marvelous prose of Jan van Ruusbroec or of Teresa of Avila, or of the poetry of Hadewych of Antwerp or John of the Cross.

What the mystic is feeling and savoring is God's intimate presence. God is near, God is within, very much in the manner of a sensible love relationship. Hence, mysticism concerns the union between God and a human being which has become conscious. For ordinary believers this relationship also exists, but on an unconscious level. Such persons know and *believe* that God dwells within them but do not experience his presence. Ruusbroec repeatedly says: "All good people have this, but *how* this takes place remains hidden from them for their entire lives, unless they are interior persons" (that is, unless they are given mystical grace). Only the mystic perceives and experiences what it means to live "in the state of grace," if we would put it in theological terms.

The perception of God's indwelling is not constant for the mystic, either. Moments of ecstatic clarity alternate with periods of dryness and darkness. Although the spiritual life never proceeds in the same manner for any two mystics, nevertheless each mystic experiences a gradual growth in intimacy with God, a growth which has its ups and downs. The mystic always looks back upon his or her past life as a "love story," a history of a

love relationship which, going from an initially strongly felt am-
orousness, through periods of abandonment and desolation,
gradually ripens to a self-forgetting love. Teresa of Avila compares the various degrees of intimacy with God to the various
rooms of a castle into which, once the threshold is crossed, a
person penetrates more deeply, growing in spiritual hiddenness.
For his part, John of the Cross compares this growth with the
ascent of a high mountain (in this instance Mount Carmel). This
"growth" has nothing to do, however, with "degrees" of increasing perfection, which could be attained by living a rigorous
life. It is merely a question of being able to affirm phenomenologically that someone who takes up God's invitation to friendship experiences something subject to growth and history.
Hence, there is no sudden leap from the initial knowledge in
faith to an experience in mystical ecstasy. Rather, it is what Thérèse of Lisieux called "the story of a soul." This story of a growing love for God, unique for each mystic, is full of unforeseen
happenings. Although spiritual writers for the most part are in
agreement with the schematic description of the way in which
God ordinarily acts with his chosen ones, the concrete story of
each mystic contains something unique. Is not the bond of love
which grows between two human beings also always something
unique? And yet its unique character does not make a general
study of the psychology, or even of the philosophy, of human
love and friendship meaningless.

Does the mystic then not run a danger of becoming an ex-
perience-starved quietist who wants to cultivate the delicate little garden of his or her own love life, but in the meantime leaves
the great field of the world's affairs lying fallow? Indeed not.
Rather, the contrary is true; that very interiority is what presses
the mystic to go outward toward others. The heart is so full of
what has been seen that the mystic "cannot but speak." In a
world which, as far as interiority is concerned, is poor in experience, it could certainly be the task of the mystic to witness to the

lost dimension of inwardness rather than to join with the powerful choir of those who, finally, are raising the hymn of social justice. Dedicating oneself to a better world includes more than commitment in the social field alone. The most conscious need is not necessarily also the most urgent one. We live, not by bread alone, but by every word from God, and *that* word often comes to us by way of the testimonials of the mystics.

Is the mystic not such an eccentric and extreme case of human psychology that mystical experiences and insights remain without any practical relevance for the ordinary believer? The mystic is as relevant for a searching believer as a piano virtuoso for an amateur musician, or as a Nobel Prize winner in literature for the average reader. If someone wants to find out how a harpsichord sounds, will not a rendition by Gustave Leonhardt, howsoever exceptional and unique his talent might be, make it much clearer than the mediocre playing of a pupil from one of our average music conservatories? Is not the essence of Christian marriage better illuminated by one of the exceptionally successful examples of it than by a description of the average couple's trials and errors? The mystic is indeed exceptional, resembling someone coming back from an inaccessible land. It does not seem to be the lot of the average person to enter this land during an entire lifetime, no matter how much it may be longed for in the best of moments. That longing is increased precisely by listening to the accounts of those who were there, and all the more so in that each believer knows that he or she is ultimately called to this still alien, but fascinating, land. The mystic is the herald of something announced for everyone, whether each individual now longs for it sensibly or not. Who takes it amiss if a pioneer has run ahead? Can anyone say that a trail-blazer, who has known and experienced more than the average person, has thereby become useless or irrelevant for humankind?

Among all the possible different ways of seeing, there are a few which touch us at our deepest level. "Thither lies truth"

(William James). "That corresponds with the way I feel," we say. "It sounds credible and cannot possibly be fiction out of the clear blue sky." The phenomenological descriptions of mystics have revealed to many people that what they experienced vaguely and embryonically has been experienced more deeply and expressed more exactly by persons greater than themselves. For these people, a mystic is not only a confirmation, but a stimulus for opening their own eyes still wider. In fact, there is much more "to see" than the average person imagines. Accounts written by mystics have already greatly enriched the inner life of many "ordinary" but clear-sighted persons. Yet, for all that, our question is still unanswered. How can a mystic, who has a rather exceptional and separate place in every religion, enrich the ordinary faith community?

Perhaps no one has more clearly described the social significance of the mystics in each great culture than the Jewish philosopher H. Bergson. He sees in mysticism one of the two sources of all morality and of all religion. He even regards the mystic as the most creative source of human progress. First of all, Bergson identifies a static, closed religion which exists in a particular moment of history in a particular culture. It consists of the sum total of convictions or dogmas and moral practices or rites. Bergson considers every social organization and morality of a given people as impossible without such religious institutions.

With this concept, Bergson stands completely in the traces of what the atheist Durkheim wrote previous to him. In our days, sociologists such as Jacques Ellul and Thomas Luckmann convincingly demonstrate that even religionless societies, if they do not want to disintegrate, call on pseudo-religions for help. Think of Nazism, Marxism, or the almost sacralized forms of nationalism which have successfully assumed the role of cementing society together in some atheistic cultures, albeit at times in a hidden way. And above all, think of the moral and cultural chaos which often arises where such "invisible religions" or irrational ideologies have totally vanished![10]

In contrast to this, Bergson characterizes still another sort of religion. Here he speaks of "dynamic, open, intuitive and mystical religion." This is religion as it is experienced and as it will go on being experienced by some privileged souls, specifically the mystics, who live in direct personal relationship with the very Source of all religious life, namely God. Are these socially irrelevant persons? Are they solitaries or marginal phenomena lacking influence on the masses or on common opinion? Quite the contrary. "These privileged ones would fain draw humanity after them; since they cannot communicate to the world at large the deepest elements of their spiritual condition, they transpose it superficially; they seek a translation of the dynamic into the static which society may accept and stabilize by education."[11] The mystic is the driving force which breathes new life into the existing moral and religious forms, and thereby, in part, changing, reforming, or ennobling them. This power derives from the direct experience of God. Static religious structures such as the Indian caste system were criticized and humanized through the religious inspiration of the mystic Gandhi. Prince Gautama broke with the privileged, royal existence which his father enjoyed in feudal Nepal and became, as a religiously-illuminated pilgrim, the "Buddha." He founded a religion which, though it later gradually took on static forms, was primarily for pariahs and for the poor. The existing religious laws of Ismel, kept stable by the scribes, were transferred by Christ onto New Testament tracks. St. Paul, whose mysticism was so clearly brought out by Albert Schweitzer, would exchange the old law for a new "law of love." According to Bergson, genuine religious progress, meaning the deepening and humanizing of existing religion rather than adaptation and modernization of its structures by sociologists or smooth administrators, has everywhere been the work of mystics. This is not hard to understand, since in essence religion is a "state of soul," not a doctrine or an organization. It is a state of soul which is always found in its purest form among these rare, great and privileged persons we call the mystics. Their spiritual life and their word act infectiously on the spiritual lives of thousands of ordinary believers. Many a great mystic's "state of soul" gets crystallized later on. In other words, it may take on the stable forms of a doctrine, a way of life and a new "mentality." This is how their dynamic religion takes on a stability which defies the passage of time. It is also the way in which what was originally the privilege of a few chosen souls becomes, in a certain sense, attainable by everyone.

The mystic, however, never stands detached from the existing religious grouping or religion. He or she is not an innovator, not a *deus ex machina* suddenly popping up out of nowhere, but has been born and bred within a particular community or Church and has inherited the language (dogmas) and practices (rites) of that community. The mystic experiences the living reality of this language and these rites, realities which have become abstract theories and matters of habit for many fellow believers. Rather than inventing new dogmas or revelations, the mystic perceives the reality behind existing expressions about God, expressions which, in fact, have grown out of earlier experiences that other privileged persons (for example, the apostles) had with God. By breathing something of the fervor which animates them into the rigid formality of existing religious groups, mystics become agents of religious transformation.

If the relationship between God and individual persons, or between God and his people, is essentially a "love story," then the principal actors in it are the mystics. "Story" implies change or growth. Consciousness of the need to change is usually reserved to the mystic, to begin with. Because of the direct relationship with God, a creative power for renewal flows forth from the mystic for the benefit of the entire community of faith. It is a power which, on the one hand, reproves whatever is false in the community of faith. On the other hand, it witnesses for the living God whom the mystic has experienced and who always transcends human forms, whether of words or of images. An acute awareness of this aspect explains the mystic's refusal to absolutize expressions about God and images of him. In this connection, Tillich speaks of the "protestant principle" present in every mystic, for the mystic "protests" against everything that comes between human persons and God. The mystic is a witness that priests, ecclesiastical authority, dogmatic formulation, the biblical word of God, sacramental rites, and other religious forms are relative means or runways along which we can approach God. But we cannot make them into absolute hypostases of God. This is the temptation into which we have fallen again and again throughout history: we began to revere things, words, or particular people as if they were God himself.

The mystic is so aware of being grasped by the direct and sensible presence of God that empty, theoretical chatter about God becomes intolerable and trying to capture God in purely human forms and things is seen as sacrilegious. Wanting to capture God in concepts is quite different, however, from pointing to him with symbols. The mystic protests against everything that falsifies the relationship between God and his human creatures or puts it in a wrong light. No wonder that many ecclesiastical "system-builders" only saw the mystic as an obstinate nuisance. Joan of Arc, John of the Cross, and Ignatius of Loyola, for example, were all prisoners of the Inquisition.

The principal task of the mystic consists in giving his or her own relationship with God a central place: "The Lord our God is one Lord; and you shall love the Lord your God . . ." (Dt 6:4). This focus helps us to see what is merely accidental in ecclesiastical structures and activities, and that these can be only a *consequence* of the religious relationship between ourselves and God. While religious structures and activities are neither unimportant nor optional, what is of primordial importance is the personal relationship with God. Wherever this is lacking or has fallen away, the only things left are hollow phrases and empty routines.

No one can be surprised that, after a period of enthusiastic chatter about a religionless, secularized Christianity, more and more believers want to let the mystic have the floor. A mystic is not someone who became so disappointed in outward activities and an unsuccessful dedication to other human beings that he or she withdrew into the peace of quiet interiority. A mystic is someone who, brim-full of the love relationship experienced with God, is sent out from that plenitude to the rest of humanity.

In one sense, the mystic stands in relation to existing religion just as a scientist stands in relation to accepted technology. No one can deny that modern nuclear physics exercises a vast influence on the concrete life of the modern man or woman who, nevertheless, has little or no idea of atomic physics and who perhaps regards it all as an abstract theory. So, too, the influence of the great mystics has been decisive for all renewals of organized religions or Churches in every age.

Finally, the mystic has an important role to play on the level of ecumenism. Since the nucleus of every religion in fact is a "state of soul," a being-moved-and-touched-interiorly-by-God, then Confessions desiring to enter into dialogue with each other must direct their focus toward what really unites them. Ultimately, this is always the experience of the same God. The rich diversity of the exterior forms given it is not so important. Outer forms given to inner experience can differ vastly from culture to culture and even from temperament to temperament. R. C. Zaehner, the English convert and specialist in the matter of Eastern religions, affirms that it is only from its mystical element that a useful dialogue between East and West can begin. This certainly does not mean that the mystical center is identical or equal in all religions. It would be a seriously simplistic rational-

ization to posit that the differences between religions can be reduced to diverse cultural forms of one and the same unique
experience of God. Such a position contains more of intellectual
sloth than of ecumenical openness.

It is not very popular at present to affirm that religions, cultures, or human beings can differ in value. Yet such differences
are evident. The different religions are not equal manifestations
of and attempts to express one and the same basic insight and
one and the same metaphysical truth. This, however, is not so a
priori. Religions are the result, formulated in language and symbol, of what went on historically between God and particular
persons (for example, Christ and his apostles) or between God
and particular cultures (for example, Yahweh and Israel). Inter-
personal encounters, like the relationships which grow from
them, can differ vastly in their respective degrees of intimacy.
This goes as much for the relationship between human beings
and God as for mutual relationships between human beings.
These encounters can lead to solid friendship, but they can also
remain coolly reserved. They can even give rise to misunderstanding. Many within as well as outside of Christianity have
"misunderstood" God. The degree of intimacy in an encounter
depends on the degree of readiness to receive a revelation about
the other. No father "reveals" his way of thinking in the same
way to all his children. No friend speaks with equal confidential-
ity to *all* of his or her acquaintances. Likewise, God does not
necessarily reveal himself in the same manner to all peoples,
nor, within one people, in the same manner to all persons.

There are people to whom God more explicitly revealed
himself (for example, the Jewish nation) just as there are persons within every religion to whom God has manifested himself
in a more sensible way (for example, the mystics). For Jews and
Christians, among others, the fact that the Word of God has revealed himself to them in a more forceful manner implies that
they have a more precise apparatus for understanding, and a

more effective religious symbolism for describing the *Ineffable*. Who can fully understand, and, especially, who can put into words the fact that God is *simultaneously* the "wholly Other" (i.e., the totally Transcendent) and yet also *intimior intimo meo* (closer to me than I am to myself), unless God, as it were, puts "the Word" himself into our mouth? Jews, Moslems and heretical Puritans saw in God for the most part the Inaccessible, the Unknowable, the one who almost crushes us with his love. Pantheists, in contrast, consider that between God and humans (hence, in religious life) a melting down process of total identification is going on. Here, the person disappears into nothingness, and is absorbed in the All. But for Jews and Christians, the person remains fully human and God remains eternally God.

Human thinking alone is unable to solve this dilemma. Human reason falls short when it comes to thinking of transcendence and immanence at the same time. The cause of this insufficiency is not lack of good will, deformation of the human mind, lack of intellectual effort, or moral malformation. The cause is merely human limitations faced with divine Mystery. When human understanding has climbed as high as nature allows it to, it then discovers that God still remains distant and inaccessible. This is the very moment (and it cannot happen earlier) when God reaches out the hand of his revealing Word. God bestows on us a language and a Word in which he expresses himself and with which we cannot only think *about* God but also *speak to* him. It is in Christ that we discover unambiguously something about the essence of God. For he who sees Christ sees the Father.

Since religion is not an irrational, chaotic condition but rather a state of soul which only expresses itself in a language, and since it was precisely an adequate language that was missing in order for the everlasting Mystery to be put into words, this "language" (the "Word of God") was given to us in the revelation of God. In his Incarnate Word, God himself gave us the key for this gateway to the Ineffable and Unthinkable. God becomes human without ceasing to be God. God is integrated immanently in humanity, without losing his transcendence on that account. Men and women, then, for their part, are called to eternal divinization, without becoming absorbed in God or in the All. Human remains human—eternally. A love experience presupposes at least two persons. To say that God is love, from all eternity, even before the creation, is only possible if there is a plurality of persons present in God. To say that the Christian views and thinks of God as "trinitarian" is an abstract way of expressing that God, in Christian perspective, was already love before we ever existed. God has always loved someone. God loves eternally.

All mystics within the great religions (Judaism, Islam, Hinduism, Buddhism, and Christianity) have not only had the "insight into" that divine life of love but also have repeatedly experienced it. Christians alone, however, have an adequate symbolism for expressing this Mystery in some intelligible way. It is in this alone that their totally unmerited advantage over the so-called nature religions consists.

Not only do all the mystics *know* that God is love; they have *experienced* it. This experience they have attempted to express in human language; that is why their witness is so enriching. It is only in mysticism that humans have ever been successful at putting into words the ineffable enigma of the relationship between God and human beings. It has been expressed, not in a language of rational abstraction, but in the living word of direct experience. This is why the mystic so often causes a rupture in the fixed thinking and speaking of every static religion. Through this beneficial rupture in the system, a new flood of life rushes to overpower the existing structures of language and life. Since all real life comes from God, it should be no surprise that the purest mystics of every great religion have all witnessed to the same thing: God is love, and God invites us to a love-response. Speaking of love, however, is something quite different from speaking of a process of absorption into the sleep of unconscious Infinity.

Do all mystics, then, repeat the same refrain over and over? No, no more than Christ was experienced by John, Luke, or Paul in identical fashion. The same person is continually experienced and understood (or at times misunderstood) by different people in many different ways. Modern theology speaks quite freely about development of dogma. But such a growth is possible only when we also assume a "development of experience." The history of Christian mysticism is nothing but the history of the experience of God. Here we are not concerned with a series of new revelations, but with a series of experiences of the God-of-Revelation with the chosen ones of his Church.

To call the mystics "chosen people" sounds rather strange in the ears of modern men and women who are allergic to every form of elitism. But God's chosen ones are not a-social. They are always sent back, burdened with a special mission, to their people. Ruusbroec never meant so much for his Flemish compatriots and even for the entire Western ecclesiastical community as when he gave up his active service as a Brussels curate in order to seek quiet in a hermitage in the Forest of Soignies. Only after that could his radiating influence over all Europe begin. As is the case for each "chosen one," his vocation was of an exceptional sort. "A bird's flight is admired, but it is neither imitated nor learned" (du Bos). The history of mysticism shows quite conclusively that the special mission of the chosen one includes the cross as an almost inseparable requisite. "Everyone to whom much is given, of him will much be required" (Lk 12:48).

To put it in biblical language, God's chosen ones are "mediators." The biblical concept of "mediator" or "intermediary" differs completely from what is called a "go-between" or "arbitrator" in modern business. This latter term generally applies to someone who seems acceptable, in spite of all, for two parties in conflict, and who can thereby bring about an agreement between the principal antagonists. In the biblical sense, however, mediators such as Abraham, Moses, and (eminently) Jesus Christ were ones so loved by the Almighty that by them and on account of them God reaches out to his people. On account of his faithful chosen ones, God draws his whole sinful people nearer to himself. On account of Moses, his "intimate friend" and spokesperson, God remains faithful to his sinful people. "For the sake of ten (just persons), I will not destroy (Sodom)" (Gen 18:32), Yahweh says to Abraham. In his chosen ones, God loves his entire people, just as, in Christ, he draws the whole world—believers and unbelievers—to himself.

The mission of the Christian minority in the world is the same as the mission of the mystic within the believing minority itself. They are temples in which God dwells in the midst of his people. The temple is not there on account of the priest. Temple and priest are there on account of God, on account of him who longs to be with his people. God's active presence for his people takes root in the mystic. Can one do more for the rest of humanity than to be a bridgehead and a mouthpiece for the Almighty and his salvation in the world? And yet the mystic is far more than a means or a channel. God's eye rests with contentment upon the mystic. This biblical saying fits the mystic far more than any other creature: "And God saw everything that he had made, and behold, it was very good" (Gen 1:31). In this sense, one can call the mystic the very crown of creation.

• 4 •

Suffering and the Experience
of Absence

"We must ask ourselves if to understand through suffering is not the capital feature as well as the daring element in our most clear-sighted mysticism."[1] The striking place which suffering occupies in the description of religious experience is not to be attributed to masochism, nor to a morbid mysticism of the cross. It is no accident that love and suffering ("passion") have something to do with each other. It is precisely the ultimate inaccessibility and the chronic absence of the beloved which makes love so "passionate" and which stimulates the lover's craving so much. When the beloved is absent or hidden, then famished, even jealous, love awakens in the most acute way. Satisfied love, on the contrary, betokens the passionlesss stillness of Nirvana rest. In opposition to the "burning heart" of the Christian seeker-after-God there stands the Buddhist waterlily of the poet Van Eeden: "Now it rests, meditating, upon the water's surface, and desires no more." But is love not a longing for two-someness rather than a satisfied oneness?

Inaccessible or impossible unity stimulates longing. By definition, God is the Incomprehensible. The experiences of the "cor irrequietum," the restless heart yearning for God, are then all the stronger the more we have tasted or have already seen something of God's attractiveness. One who has never made a friend does not know what it means to experience someone's absence. The suffering of absence is a painful but rich and stirring state of soul. This is the very paradox of love: the more intimately the beloved has penetrated my heart, the more I am going to feel his or her absence. The more I taste of love (and this is not given to everyone, just as it appears that faith, too, is not given to everyone), the greater my thirst becomes. Not missing God at all, being able to get along very well without God, is only the lot of those who haven't the least glimmer of a notion who God is. One must have come across God sometime, at least, for one to have an idea of what "desolation," i.e., being left alone, can mean. One must have seen trees, houses, and fertile fields in order to appreciate the dryness of the desert. "Experiencing the desert" is not the same thing as "experiencing nothing." Likewise, the feeling of God's absence is something different from religious sterility or godlessness. "We sing only of absent things" (Valéry).

Absence does not mean non-existence. In literature, the experience of a friend's absence appears to be a very inspiring experience. It was only when Elvira was no longer there that Lamartine wrote his most moving verses about her. In Hadewych's mystical poetry, too, the lover is most vehemently moved

"When he is *without*
His love, for whom he longs
And he does not possess
The one by whom he lives."[2]

As a believer, Hadewych often feels that she is "far from home, in a foreign land." Filled with homesickness she yearns for him with whom she knows she is "at home": God. Hence the experience of God is not a continual feeling of his presence. Among all believers, one of the most gripping of religious experiences is that of feeling God's painful *absence*. For many of our contemporaries God has become undiscoverable. God is the great Absent. He is, perhaps, still quite acceptable as an idea: people "believe in the existence of a God." But they no longer experience his actual Presence in this world. What is worse, many consider the very possibility of such an experience as an illusion they have outgrown. In any case, to conceive of God as absent seems to be a more popular view than to experience his presence, an experience which is at best considered a luxury enjoyed by a few reasonable people.

The question is whether this religious vacuum is experienced more as a lack or as finally being liberated from a constrictive figment of our childhood imagination. The first instance is a necessary phase in the religious maturation process. Every believer, at one time or another, proposes such considerations as these: "God used to mean something in my life. But now I have lost all feeling for him. No matter how I pine for the experiences of long ago, they seem to belong to the past." Moments of night-like darkness come into every love relationship. But only one who has seen daylight really knows what night is. Not even the greatest saints were spared this experience of emptiness.

Just such a situation of suffering from God's absence made Christ cry out: "My God, my God, why hast thou forsaken me?" (Mt 27:46). Thérèse of Lisieux, for her part, lived many years of spiritual aridity and blindness. Anyone who reads the account of her interior experiences is struck by the fact that the saint experienced God's painful absence far more than his sensible presence. To her superior, she soberly wrote: "I must appear to you as a soul filled with consolations and one for whom the veil of faith is almost torn aside; and yet it is no longer a veil for me, it is *a wall* which reaches right up to the heavens and covers the starry firmament. One would have to travel through this dark tunnel to understand its darkness."[3] About the many saints who were mystically graced by the experience of God's presence, she wrote: "I then understood what the saints are saying and these states which they have so often experienced. As for myself, I felt it but once, and for only an instant; then I immediately fell back into my habitual aridity." The experience described by Thérèse is not that God is absent, but that his sensible presence disappears at times. This brings about an experience of deep pain from the supposed abandonment and from longing for the Beloved. To experience *nothing* on the religious level is a totally different thing. Can we ever explain what love is if the person to whom we speak claims to have been feeling just fine for years, living totally wrapped up in his or her own self?

But present-day religious emptiness can also assume yet subtler forms. Many affirm that whatever used to touch them most deeply now leaves them cold and no longer speaks to them. It appears that they have lost all feeling for that which used to have deep value for them. Experience is cut off from them. Everything having to do with God becomes quiet, so quiet in fact that many are inclined to wonder if he is still really there. God no longer seems just "absent"; he has been lost and risks being totally forgotten. Who ever continues to hunt for what cannot be found? Is not this stillness, however, a characteristic phenomenon of every human relationship? Is not the thunder of the first encounter always followed by a quiet time either of maturation into faithful love or else a disappearance into the nothingness of transitory? A relationship traveling only on the steam of remarkable experiences never reaches the stable shores of faithful love. Without the dreadful night of suffering from absence, faithful friendship remains an unknown land. We have to miss a certain friend badly a few times before we can discover who this friend really is.

The way to God, just like the road to the promised land, necessarily leads through the desert of monotony. Can the discovery of an oasis be a significant experience for someone who never stayed for a long time in the desert? "Experience has become a magic word in our days, a word in vogue, rated high on the market of modern sensibility. The hunger for experience, a keen longing for 'life,' the cult of new experiences, a sort of universal curiosity about the strange and exotic, the fear that we might miss something: these are the most striking characteristics of modern man with his endemic dread of boredom. We have to taste, try, and experience everything. It is the principle of maximizing existence by multiplying contacts and relationships, by the intensive use of signs and objects, by the systematic exploitation of all possibilities of pleasure. We have to try everything. . . . You never know if such and such a contact, such and such an experience, might not get a 'sensation' out of us."[4] But when the object of my experience is a person, human or divine, then the decisive question immediately comes up: What am I really looking for, the person of my beloved with *his* or *her* feelings, longings, and uniqueness, or *my* experience of the beloved? Am I looking for my spouse or am I looking for an erotic sensation? Am I looking for God, or am I seeking purely my devotion, my spiritual rest, or my psychological well-being? Am I seeking the other, or am I seeking my experience? If the latter is true, I may indeed *speak* of love, but what I am looking for is myself. Do I have my partner's person in mind, or am I looking for my socio-psychological comfort? It is one thing to be apprehensive about our own loneliness, and quite another thing to be mindful of the happiness of another (my "other").

As soon as my attention shifts from the person of the other to concentrate on my own experience of the other's presence, the very core of the love encounter has already been slain. What I am doing then is what Augustine said about himself before his conversion to God: "Amabam amare"—I loved to love. I loved falling in love. "What they (Tristan and Isolde) love is love and being in love. . . . Their need of one another is in order to be aflame, and they do not need one another as they are. What they need is not one another's presence, but one another's absence."[5] If the importance of religion ebbs away as soon as the felt experience of God no longer fills the "pious" person, then that person has never experienced faith, only devotion. Relishing devotion has no more to do with belief than sexual awakening for an adolescent has to do with married love. To seek experience for the sake of experience is to seek oneself. To seek the other on account of that other is to experience love. Jacques de Bourbon-Busset attributes the failure of many relationships to confusion about this. "Our era placed the accent more on the nature of the relationship than on the poles which that relationship unites."[6] Applied to the relationship with God, it goes as follows: "Only one thing interests the modernist or liberal theologian: religious experience and our consciousness of it, the reality . . . of the first cause (God) being clearly subordinated to the very intensity of the experience. Whence the immanentism (outright or confused) which characterizes this theology."[7] It is a theology which is taken up with human psychology more than with the reality of God, with my emotional state more than with the person of God.

Many a lover says: "In all my dealings, I am only moved by my love for you." In reality, such a lover means: "I am driven by my spontaneous yearnings and by my hunger for experience." And many a Christian says: "When I speak and act in such and such a way, then it is out of faith." What is really meant is: "I am acting out of *my* principles and out of *my* ingrained tradition." But true love and true faith move one in the opposite direction. Levinas, in speaking of those who want not only to enjoy, use and possess their partners but also to love and respect them in their otherness, finds that the presence of the "other" puts a check on their spontaneity.[8] Every normal person spontaneously goes looking for a love experience, but few rein in their egocentric desires with an eye to their partner's happiness. Many discover in themselves a need for religion, but few have any notion that the way to God follows the way of the cross and through the desert of emptiness and absence. "Those who have grace feel replete with presence, and not of void. This presence was evidently preceded *by a sort of emptiness,* which is not *the* emptiness, but a way of setting non-essential things aside in order to approach the essential," says Ionesco.[9]

The cross always means a disowning of our "I." What once was my self-contained property becomes a shared possession when I love. As long as a child hangs on to a toy, the child cannot receive anything more valuable from his or her mother. Only by letting go of the plaything and stretching out a greedy hand to ask for something more is the child ready to receive it. In suffering, God takes something away from us in order to free us for more essential things. Pain will often make us let go when we do not do so of our own volition. Suffering is a transformation process. A person passes from hanging on to things to sharing in love. We are always invited to do this, but can become embittered and refuse the invitation, since God cannot force anyone to the joy of love.

Even more painful than the experience of emptiness and absence is dread. Dread constricts our awareness and limits our horizons. One in such a state snatches at anything, looking for a firm hold or protection. In the life of nearly all religious people, the role of the experience of dread has been remarkably great. There are two kinds of dread. In the first place, there is the dread which is nothing more than a question of innate temperament having its roots in a person's physical constitution: a tendency toward high blood pressure, susceptibility to nervous tension, and little resistance against the overwhelming urges of emotional life. Many have to face life with this sort of dread, just as others face it with an especially sensitive stomach, a weak nervous system, or asthmatic lungs. Since this sort of dread stems from physical factors, all this has little to do with spiritual life and can be greatly helped by physical means such as yoga, sports, or chemical tranquillizers.

On a much deeper level, however—and this is why it has to do with religious witness—at times a person can have the feeling of being abandoned spiritually, of having lost his or her orientation, or, as far as faith is concerned, coming up against a blank wall. Kierkegaård describes such a dread as "coming up against an empty consciousness," in other words, as experiencing no more than the emptiness of one's own "I." The soul is like a radio which no longer receives any programs, and because of that produces no sound other than its own monotonous buzzing. Consciousness is like two millstones which, for want of grain, grind each other to pieces. Thrown back upon one's own resources, a person void of relationships experiences nothing but emptiness. "Subjectivity means hospitality," says Levinas. As soon as I have no more guests inhabiting my heart, my subjectivity degenerates into emptiness. This is the sort of abandonment which made Christ sweat blood "out of dread." Left alone even by his most intimate disciples, he also no longer experienced God's presence: "My God, my God, why hast thou forsaken me?" It is the same experience ascribed to Job: forsaken by God, he was left to his lot by everyone else.

In this condition of dread, two types of reactions are possible: faith or doubt. First of all, based on previous experience, one can keep on believing and hoping against what immediately appears to have no future. In his last discourse, the Lord gave the admonition: "Let not your hearts be troubled neither let them be afraid." He knew what frightful, dreadful experiences lay in store for all of his disciples. Four times he emphasized: "I tell you this now, before it takes place, that when it does take place, you may believe. . . . I have said all this to you to keep you from falling away (i.e., on account of the experiences of dread,

suffering and death)."[10] Living out of experience in no way
means denying or forgetting all our past and building only on
the immediate experiences of the present. This is the way of
doubt, the way of a person who trusts solely in what is seen, felt,
and heard *now,* of a person who, because the sun is now hiding
behind the clouds, no longer believes that there is a sun, and has
even forgotten that he or she ever saw the sun.

Luther said: "Difficulty teaches us to take notice of the
word." Someone beset by doubt and dread, therefore, is in a
condition to feel the range of God's previously spoken word. In
the pain of being abandoned, the word that had been withheld
becomes real. The word, experience concretized, is the pilgrimage through the emptiness experience of the horizonless desert
of life. No mystic is spared dread, *the* most painful experience
imaginable. John of the Cross calls it "night."[11] This night is
"bitter and terrible to the senses," that is, for psychological experience. "This affliction owes not so much to the aridities they
undergo as to their fear of having gone astray. Since they do not
find any support or satisfaction in good things, they believe
there will be no more spiritual blessing for them and that God
has abandoned them." "It is God who works in (the soul)."

What is it that God is bringing about in the soul through
this "night"? Little by little he wants to give it an eye for an entirely new type of experience. He wants "to lead (the soul) on to
a higher degree of divine love." To do that, he first weans the
soul from the satisfaction or consolation it used to get from the
things of God as well as from creatures. None of this speaks to
the soul as it used to. Its attention is more on its own suffering
and on its anxiety about going backward spiritually. But this is
how the soul is almost imperceptibly sensitized for a whole new
understanding of God's presence, an experience which John of
the Cross says is "far removed from all these other gratifications
of beginners which are very palpable and sensory."[12]

But, in fact, is not this talk of "intangible experience" a contradiction in terms or non-essential caviling? A comparison may make it clear that this is not the case. Who has never known that awful feeling of boredom, even of revulsion, upon seeing one's old toys and childish amusements? The crisis of puberty leads one gradually to open up to *new* objects which begin little by little to attract one's attention. Between the childish enthusiasm of the past and the sphere of interest of the adult, there lies the heavy vacuum of the adolescent who can no longer enjoy the old and who rejects it as childishness. "All things are too tight for me; I am so broad." These are the words of an anonymous poet who has grown beyond an enthusiasm for sensible devotion and who hungers for a more essential experience. Taken on a profane level, these words just fit the painful state of an adolescent. Is it not the adolescent's impression that the old now seems too constricting and too insignificant to really provide satisfaction anymore?

Just as much as that adolescent, the person who is growing religiously needs this monotonous vacuum in order to acquire a taste for solid food in place of spiritual milk. Weaning a child has always been a painful undertaking. The infant must have experienced a fear of dying of hunger. Similarly, the night of the senses is a spiritual weaning on the road to religious adulthood. "Undergo it passively, endure it, remain calm, and do not undertake anything," runs John of the Cross' advice to those who are steered by God through the night of his absence. Their most dangerous temptation would involve taking over the helm themselves: trying a new method of prayer, or looking toward different techniques of meditation or new practices or more modern formulas—if only to escape from the monotony of interior emptiness. Has the Church, in the course of its history, ever hummed so much from the rush of activities, new organizational forms and attempts at "aggiornamento" as in our times? Is not external busy-ness often the sign of internal boredom or insecurity? Noisy busy-ness and absorbing activities are the cheapest, and possibly the most used, narcotics to extinguish the gnawing pain of internal hollowness. The popular notion is that unless people "do" something, they will not "experience" anything— ergo, their frantic activity.

The worker is alienated from his or her own work, complained Marx, and more and more modern people complain with him about that. But we forget that there is an even more painful alienation. One can be alienated from one's own interior. Many workers (business people, politicians, priests, etc.) in fact appear so attached to and enslaved by their objective work that they lose any feeling for their own spiritual life. If the automobiles on the assembly line where you work leave you cold, it is less serious than if you become alienated from God who dwells within you, from the spouse who is one flesh with you, and from any form of personal reflection or interior life. Moreover, someone who no longer experiences anything as far as intimacy with spouse and children is concerned runs the risk of clinging to a job which absorbs all personal time and attention. It is just the priest or sister whose prayer-life is running dry who risks becoming the slave of "apostolic" activities. But an apostolate is more a consequence of a plenitude than a means against interior emptiness.

There is one type of emptiness which is the consequence of superficiality, but there is also one which is a road toward spiritual deepening. It is this second emptiness which concerns John of the Cross when he speaks of the "taste of nothingness" or of "spiritual nudity." He endures painful experience because he sees in it the only tunnel offering passage toward higher mountains. Not to fill this salutary emptiness with superficial stuffing is only possible for one who knows higher values than personal immediate psychological gratification *now*. For someone greedy for gratification, the pain of emptiness is *the* enemy to flee. For one who loves, pain of felt absence is the inevitable shadow which the mountain peak casts upon the climber's path. The mountain-climber's joy lies in the ascent to the peak, not in sitting up there for a long time, thanks to a mechanical cable car! We can liken religious experience to Eurydice: once it is grasped, it is lost, for good. "Every wish to experience happiness, to have it at one's beck and call—instead of *being in a state* of happiness as though by grace—must instantly produce an intolerable sense of want."[13]

Loving is a state of "being," not a question of "having." We *are* directed toward the other, but we *possess* no one. Perhaps we *have* convictions, but we *are* believing. We do not *have* a spiritual life or a high degree of perfection, but we *are* yearning for God. This should be a warning for those looking for richer religious experiences, e.g., "for a Mass we can *get* something out of," more than for God who, for the Christian, always comes "like the Bridegroom at *night.*"

Speaking about God's absence always remains a question of speaking about pain, hunger, and suffering. For every Christian, the pathway to God runs along the dreadful agony of Gethsemani to the forsakenness of Calvary. The Stoic accepts pain cold-bloodedly as an unavoidable evil while throwing the protective cloak of reason over any affective life. The Christian, however, knows that in itself suffering can be just as sterile as it can be fruitful. As long as it receives no positive meaning, suffering remains an undifferentiated experience. Suffering never bears a positive meaning intrinsically. By nature, it is destructive and absurd. Suffering receives a meaning only from the human response to it. No one ever gave suffering a deeper meaning than did Christ on his cross. Henceforth, the cross becomes the symbol of "suffering with a meaning." The cross means "suffering with faith." "To take up one's cross" means to accept suffering and to see it as a passageway to a higher form of life and of happiness.

But the believer never seeks suffering. To set oneself on fire, like Jan Palach of Hungary, making a heroic spectacle of oneself, is a practice which is known in Buddhist monasticism but which has nothing in common with Christian spirituality. To flog oneself may be proper to Moslem fakirs, but it has nothing to do with Gospel Christianity. In Christian perspective, the believer should strive by every possible means to avoid and to overcome suffering. Just as a healthy body protects itself against illness with antibodies, so also the healthy soul defends itself against psychological sufferings.

The Christian is not a neurasthenic maniac. Faith has as little to do with masochism as penance has to do with arousing pain artificially. The believer lets unavoidable suffering do its work in the center of his heart, like streaming rains over a seeded field. If a painful experience cannot be overcome, the believer not only endures it with resignation but recognizes the cross in it, finds real meaning, not happenstance, in it. For the Christian, "bearing one's cross" means to see a meaning in unavoidable suffering. The Christian knows that the cross is not the end and that death will never have the last word. For the believer, the real "Omega point" is personal resurrection, and the principal feast is Easter, not Good Friday. The believer accepts painful experience; the masochist, on the other hand, stimulates and cultivates it. The believer bears suffering out of love-for-the-Other. The masochist, however, experiences pain in order to distill a morbid elixir of perverse pleasure from it. Basically, both believer and masochist are looking for an "other," the former out of being in love with thoughts and feelings focused on the Beloved, the latter out of a need for attention and pity from others and a preoccupation with a negative world of personal experience. The believer is not someone who looks for pain, thinking to find salvation in it. But when the believer experiences pain, it is accepted as a cross which weighs on the shoulders and which is borne patiently as long as the Lord asks it. The cross is never fashioned by the believer. It is not "my personal effort," but a temporal testing by him. The purpose is not the annihilation but the ennoblement of the cross-bearer. Like gold in the crucible, or like a seed bursting forth into a plant in the fields, the believer is not absorbed by the Other. Rather, the believer knows that suffering leads to being taken up and received as a genuine friend. The believer's happiness, then, does not come from the "exhausting and delicious awareness of failure"[14] but from the realization of having been called to total self-fulfillment in love. There is no ignoring the fact that the way to happiness is filled with shadowy twistings and purifying downpours. But rather than reveling in this, the believer's attention is on the radiant face of the Beloved.

What exactly is the sufferer purified from? From self-awareness, as the masochist thinks? From passions, as the Buddhist thinks? From the material world, as the Hindu thinks? From freedom, as Dostoevsky's worried Grand Inquisitor thought? Is it thinkable that God would want to purify his human creatures from the noblest gift with which he endowed them at creation? Was it given only to be brutally withdrawn? Rather than masochistic human beings, are we faced with a sadistic God?

Pain always indicates a disturbance in the organism. Pain calls for healing, not for amputation. The sick head does not beg: "Chop me off!" The sore eye does not sigh: "Pluck me out!" An eye wants to see clearly once again, just as a broken leg wants to walk supplely once more. A person united with God sees in the soul's pain a sure sign that God is at work, like a vine-grower doing needed pruning. We do not always understand what is happening to us. We experience pain, but believe at the same time that what happens to us is neither accidental nor purposeless. We do not artificially maintain that pain. Rather, we fight against it when possible, and are patient and bear it when it is unavoidable. Even in pain, the believer experiences something of God. God purifies those whom he loves. But the question remains: purified of what?

Suffering purifies us from things of secondary importance

and directs us to what is essential. That is to say, it purifies us from that which God, our Creator, regards as superfluous (but to which we are often inclined to remain fanatically attached) in order to direct us toward that which constitutes our true and lasting happiness, according to our Creator who knows us better than we do ourselves. Hence, the cross points us toward that for which God has created us. We can, it is true, refuse this orientation and keep going our own way according to our recipe for happiness. Augustine vividly summarizes God's plan with the words: "Thou hast made us for thyself, O Lord!" Therefore, we shall find neither rest nor happiness as long as we keep ourselves intent on non-essentials in place of starting out on the route leading to what our nature even unconsciously seeks, namely God.

A person passively undergoes this purification process in the suffering which is unintentionally experienced. This should often be supplemented actively with some ascesis. Ascesis is the effort one freely enters into in order to get rid of trash, insofar as it is a hindrance for what is Essential. Ascesis is not a technique which can lead us to the footsteps of the Essential. Ascesis is a practice proper to those who have already discovered and tasted the Essential. Ascesis is a process of detachment, flowing from a great attachment to life, to true life. But the way never begins with detachment from things of accidental or secondary importance which then leads us to a new attachment to what is of essential importance. The process works in quite the opposite way. First we discover the "treasure hidden in the field." Only then do we "go and sell" everything to which we were previously attached. It is all done with our eyes on Something we have *found* and not on Something for which we are still looking. The one who discovers the treasure hidden in the field goes forth and sells everything to which he or she had been attached.

And so, it is never thanks to ascetical effort that we discover the Essential. Once one has been seized by God, the futilities of life have no more meaning. We are freed from them. But since this feeling of being seized by God is not constantly sustained at the same intensity, we risk being sporadically fascinated by mundane non-essentials. Control is necessary in order to keep the rudder directed toward our freely-chosen goal, especially when we are sailing near beckoning Sirens.

If Augustine's statement that "God created man with an innate desire for himself" is true, then why do so terribly few people yearn consciously for God, and why then do so many throw themselves so enthusiastically and dependently into what we might call "non-essential futilities"? Does not the real status of the "human condition" plainly show us that the human heart, in contrast with a compass which always points north, is by no means spontaneously looking for God? Is Clavel right, then, when he pessimistically states that 'the human spirit (is) naturally and basically turned away from God," and, worse yet, that "grace is against nature . . . God tries first of all to change our being"?[15]

Such a notion would be a slap in the face for the Creator. Anyone who sees human beings as "essentially turned away from God" sees the human person as a freak. First, God creates humans. After that, he notices that his creation is fundamentally wrong. God, then, has to "change" what he created if he wants to make it possible for humans to love him ("grace"). Seen in this perspective, creation was a mistake which, thanks be to God, is rectified by a second intervention, namely the "redemption" or the "incarnation." God, who is love, would thus have made human beings with a sort of inevitable hereditary punishment. Can a person hurt an artist more deeply than by looking at the artist's creation and saying: "If it is going to be good, it has to be fundamentally changed"?

The analogy does not hold perfectly, for at birth the human person as creation by God is not "finished." The sole fact of biological birth does not make the person complete. Rather, he or she is a project, a task. Now the process that Teilhard de Chardin called "hominization" must begin, phylogenetically as well as ontogenetically. In other words, the phenomenon of the being we call human who has been on earth for six hundred thousand years is not yet perfect. Culturally and even biologically, that being will still change a lot. The human phenomenon continues to "evolve." Whether that being will become "more human" or will degenerate does not depend solely upon biological and cosmic factors; this shall also be essentially determined by the level of humanism and morality that will characterize the human of tomorrow.

The individual person too, at birth, is only beginning the creation-process. He or she must grow toward, with the possibility of growing away from, that for which the person was created by God. God's intention for the human created by him is evidently not: "Stay who you are now and keep intact what you received." God's vocation for the individual rather sounds like this: "Become gradually what you can, and ennoble what you received as nature." A human is not a pure creation by God alone. An individual becomes what he or she aims at and puts into life.

A person can also take an "inhuman" way. No horse could ever live "unhorsely"; an animal always evolves spontaneously. Where human growth is taking place, however, there is more going on than biological evolution. On the one hand, an impulse for good is alive, leading toward self-surrender in love. On the other hand, however, there is also an inclination to evil, to being wrapped up in the self out of anxiety. It is certainly a natural move for the individual to trustingly grasp the hand offered by God or by other humans. Yet, deep in the same person there are the roots of childish fear of any "other." There lurks in each of us an anxiety response which urges us, rather than to take up a proffered love relationship with its unforeseen risks, to take cover wrapped up in ourselves. Freud and Adler respectively discovered in the deepest levels of the human soul an egocentric and direct search for pleasure and a ruthless individual drive for self-affirmation. For St. John, too, "natural man," i.e., the human for whom the *possibility* of love has not yet become a *reality* through a genuine encounter with the Other, has a tendency to appropriate everything to himself. For John, "all that is in the world" is "lust of the flesh" (libidinous sexuality), "lust of the eyes" (self-affirmation), and "pride of money" (inclination toward possessiveness) (1 Jn 2:16). This sort of "world" is the core of what unfortunately has been called "original sin." This is an unfortunate term because this aspect of the human condition concerns neither a sin (it is not a voluntary act) nor something hereditary (it is not something taken over from a previous race or left from earlier times). It is rather a disturbing thrust in each person, a spontaneous ever-present anxiety reflex of muddling along and turning back upon oneself for fear of the risk of love. In other words, there exists in each of us an inclination not only to self-surrender but also to self-restraint.

This latter tendency is certainly not perverse. It is neither corrupt nor perverted by nature. It is no more than a necessary, prudent protection against spiritual and physical prostitution. One does not give oneself away to just anyone, especially not on the spiritual level. Loving one's neighbor "as oneself" is excluded for the one who denies all warm selfhood. Love presupposes personality and intimacy. This natural desire for protecting one's own "inner self," however, can be pernicious whenever this impulse becomes overriding and blocks the much subtler desire for self-surrender. Reticence then degenerates into a barricaded egocentrism. Love gets cut off by dread. As Hammarskjöld put it, the misery begins as soon as the necessary self-love prevails over the much more basic desire for self-surrender. "Original sin," then, is the tension which is never definitely overcome between anxious self-concern on the one hand and the risk of outgoing love on the other.

From birth on, we have the potential to disappropriate ourselves of ourselves in order to turn toward another in love. This step toward the "other" will always be felt as a risk before which one understandably hesitates. Egocentric drives seeking their own center inevitably set to work and put on the brakes. If a person is unwilling to give in to the natural drive for self-restraint, then a suitable ascesis must be used to gain freedom from what used to be called "self-love" and what is now called "individualism" or "narcissism."

But in addition to self-imposed asceticism there is also the cross. This latter is laid on a person's shoulders *by God.* The cross will call, but not compel, a person back to order again every time there is a temptation to seek happiness in oneself.

Because life is a "gift" signifying an invitation to enter into relationship, everything goes awry whenever we want to appropriate that life for ourselves and trick others out of something. When this happens, and this anxiety reflex of our hand closing and withdrawing itself will reappear again and again, then God warns us through his cross. The cross means expropriation. With the cross God heals and frees us from being wrapped up in ourselves. From the cross the Lord extended his hand in invitation to the two men crucified with him. The "good thief" grasped the hand that extended the happiness of paradise to him. The other turned his head away in hopeless refusal. He ended his life wrapped up in himself.

The word from the self-revealing God thaws the natural anxiety of human beings who feel vulnerable, naked, and insecure. By nature frightened of other humans ("homo homini lupus"), the one who hears God's word learns that reality is less terrifying than it otherwise appears. Such an individual experiences reality as an invitation to life outside the shell of loneliness.

Painful experiences continually force us to consider what we now hold in our tight grasp: the hand of the Beloved, or the tinsel of transitory ownership. The pain of the sober cross is bearable only for the one who recognizes that God never takes something out of our hand unless it be to make space for a more precious gift. God squeezes no one's hand tightly unless it be to draw that hand closer to himself. The fact that a hand filled with the toys of this world feels this more painfully prompted the Lord to say in his concern: "Woe to you rich, for you hold in your hand already what really consoles you."

• 5 •

Various Ways of Expressing God

It is a difficult task to define "religion" without ambiguity. The word contains almost as many meanings as there are religions. Are Buddhism and Confucianism religions? Or is it preferable to call them moralities or wisdoms? The answer depends on what is understood by "religion."

In his book *Varieties of Religious Experience,* William James starts out by using a concept of religion that had become classical, a concept that in general seems to fit Christianity as well as the other great religions. There "religion" means the ensemble of a person's feelings, experiences, and conscious states, insofar as that person is convinced that he or she exists in relationship to something "divine." In the human consciousness, there often seems to be a feeling of a Presence which makes a person say: there is Something deeper, more inclusive and more powerful than everything that continually proclaims itself as "reality" via my normal senses. There is Something which totally surpasses or "transcends" everything else. People of every culture and age have always maintained that they have felt such a thing in privileged moments. Hence it is something that oversteps the bounds of the normal or ordinary.

Yet this "Something" does not stand altogether apart from the common reality of this world. Transitory things and one's own ego become relativized in the light of this Absolute. One's "ego," humankind, and the whole cosmos are understood as "depending on" and "pointing to" this Absolute. The latter therefore gives everything a "relative" place and value. For the religious person, humanity and the world are essentially "regional," i.e., not to be understood in isolation. While the Absolute surpasses everything, it also stands in relationship to everything. Moreover, it can arouse a colorful array of emotional states in a religious person: feelings of fear, awe, enthusiasm, guilt, or desire. Just as an unexpected guest can arouse quite divergent reactions in a given group, ranging for example from undisguised resentment to surprised joy, so also the reaction of those who feel confronted by the Transcendent is colored by factors such as their personal past, emotional state, intellectual milieu, and the accidental circumstances in which this religious experience took place.

Rudolph Otto has demonstrated that the Transcendent always presents itself as simultaneously "tremendum" and "fascinosum." It is a reality which, on the one hand, inspires awe and fear, but, on the other, attracts a person in a mysterious way. God obliges us to stay at a respectful distance, while at the same time he fascinates us irresistibly. We feel fear and even guilt on account of our own littleness, and yet a peaceful trust in the Almighty, too. Respectful gravity and spontaneous enthusiasm go hand in hand. If the former feeling is dominant in Jansenistic belief, the greatest of the Christian saints have always placed stronger emphasis upon the latter aspect. The proportion not only differs from religion to religion (in Islam a fearsome distance is dominant) but also, within a given confession, from person to person. While Calvin saw God as the Awesome One, Thérèse of Lisieux recognized him as a nearby Father.

Aside from the separate case of the mystic, the Transcendent is always experienced "mediately." The divine Mystery manifests itself in creation or through certain events or phenomena, that is, indirectly through "means" or links. The Supernatural reveals itself through nature becoming transparent. It is beyond ordinary human powers of perception to experience God without some intermediary. The question is: *Where* do religious people think they find traces of God?

Primitive peoples seem to find God most often in whatever is seen as exceptional, inexplicable, shocking, dangerous, anxiety-producing, and impure. An eclipse of the sun, the sudden cure of a sick person, the outbreak of a deadly epidemic such as the plague, a lengthy drought, blood, or a corpse: these are possible phenomena in which primitive peoples always were inclined to see gods or spirits at work. These are also phenomena about which the same people often besought an intervention of the gods by sacrifices and prayers. For primitive peoples, God is the explanation of the humanly inexplicable. God is brought in when natural causes, causes which seem familiar and understandable, do not seem sufficient to explain the strangeness of an event. Since modern science is constantly reducing the sphere of the inexplicable, primitive forces of religion have less and less ground to build upon. The lucid believer prefers to seek God in the mystery which surges up *behind* everything which at first sight appears explainable scientifically.

Faced with the Transcendent, people in their respective religions have taken on three sorts of attitudes. We find *something* of these three attitudes in all religions, but the proportions of the three elements can vary widely. If the first or second attitude is typical of primitive religions, then the emphasis in most great religions is placed on the third attitude. First of all, we can declare that the places where the Transcendent is to be found are "taboo." We keep our hands off it, respectfully. A series of carefully outlined rules assure immunity against numinous infection.

Second, we can try to use the "magical" powers concealed in the Transcendent for our own practical purposes. A person focused on magic carries out mysterious rites upon objects in which he thinks divine powers are concealed, so that healing, rain, or some human good may result.

Finally, we can try to come "into relationship" with the Transcendent. Even in the case of the great religions, certain taboos or anxieties about impure "things" do crop up, and as a rule a dose of magic is available or a ritual practice is used in order to get some control of the Transcendent. Nevertheless, what is dominant here is the desire to enter into relationship with God. No human relationship is thinkable without there being at least some trace of taboo or without some implication of "using" the other. However, religious reformers have repeatedly protested whenever such secondary phenomena of superstitious taboos or magical practices were obscuring the relationship with God.

The relationship between the human person and God, that is, "religion" in the third sense of the word and the sense to which we shall henceforth limit ourselves here, can in turn be experienced in several ways. In fact, relationship with God can attain varying degrees of intimacy and intensity.

Already in the second century, Christian writers such as Lactantius and Tertullian explained the word "religio" etymologically, as derived from "re-ligari": it is continually (*re-*) being bound (*ligari*) to God in an intimate relationship of Person to person. This etymology, though incorrect,[1] is still historically significant, for it explains what Christians centuries ago understood by "religion." For Christians, the religious person has always been someone "bound to God" rather than someone ritually pure, self-disciplined, or convinced of all sorts of dogmas. In contemporary theological jargon, the word "religious" is generally reduced to a pejorative anachronism. Impersonal terms such as the Transcendent, Sacral, Absolute or Numinous, and the "deepest Ground" of "Being itself" sound more modern. The use of the impersonal "it" in place of the personal pronoun "he" speaks for itself in this connection. The religious reality is preferably kept as much as possible in vague and abstract terms, for human beings still know so terribly little about it.

The basic problem with which all great religious writers have wrestled is the question of how God can be conceived as at once totally transcendent and totally immanent. On the one hand we have some knowledge of the unbridgeable chasm which separates us from the totally surpassing Almighty One (Transcendence), but on the other hand we know the same God as present *in* this world, indeed in our very soul (Immanence). It is only since "the Word became flesh and dwelt among us" (Jn 1:14) (i.e., since Christian revelation) that the linkage between transcendence and immanence has become really possible for human language. It is in Christ that the transcendent God enters immanently *into* humanity. In Christ we reach the Transcendent God and we genuinely come into contact with the "totally Other." Since Christ, we know that the relationship between God and ourselves must be regarded as a love-relationship between two genuine but not necessarily equal persons. If the essence of the Trinitarian mystery is mutual love between persons, then, since Christ, we know that we are called to be taken up within that life of love. We are created in order to love God and to be eternally loved by him. In fact, I feel that I am continually more one (immanence) with the one I love. Nevertheless, this other does not swallow me up. I do not disappear in the other, since that would mean the end of every love experience. It is the other's very otherness (transcendence) which insatiably stimulates my desire for unity and togetherness.

"Consciousness of oneself as yearning to grasp everything,

disappointed at being unable to reach it, is, then, an amorous consciousness."[2] Independently from the historical revelation in Christ, humankind through its greatest religious minds has never ceased trying to approach the mystery of simultaneous transcendence and immanence as adequately as possible. Throughout the ages, this relationship has been conceived and put into words in very diverse ways, going from an almost agnostic feeling of "something incomprehensible" within or behind sensible reality, to a passionate desire for "Someone" regarded as a love partner.

Though we risk doing violence to the highly complex reality of the religious phenomenon by a much too schematic classification, we will nevertheless try here to distinguish five types of religious experience.

In milieus where all conscious experience of God is held as a strictly impossible remnant from an outmoded and scientific *Weltanschauung,* we find a vague notion of "Something" which apparently transcends what is normal and rational. This we can characterize as an "agnostic-irrational experience of transcendence." Second, we distinguish a purely natural, psychologically explainable experience of absoluteness. In other words, human psychology does not seem to be constantly bound to time and space. There are privileged moments in which a person has the feeling, which may or may not be illusory, of going "outside space and time," moments of ecstasy or rapture which should not necessarily be relegated to the domain of parapsychology or the preternatural. Third, we find the experience of being taken up into the All of nature or of the Cosmos, or at least the intense desire for it. Fourth, we find people who have a feeling of discovering their "real self" within the (worthless) shell of their historically transitory "ego." Finally, then, in a later chapter we will treat of the Christian experience of God in which God comes as a Person with a call to love.

1. The "Agnostic" Experience of Transcendence

Some agnostics have the realization in privileged moments that beyond the limits of the humanly knowable there could exist still another Reality. Anyone who talks about "beyond the limits" is already ipso facto speaking about Something transcending the closed "this-sidedness" of humans. Meanwhile, agnostics may keep on hammering on the assertion that we cannot know anything meaningful about that "other side" and thus cannot express anything about it. They are annoyed by the verbosity of many believers when they speak about God. They seem to dispose of so many theological "facts" and "certainties" that the Transcendent is reduced from an unapproachable Mystery to an impersonal entity.[3] The agnostic experiences no specific Being in addition to other beings, but rather a question mark, a void, a "no-thing."

In fact, no limitations can be set up for the Transcendent; it is "unlimited" and surpasses all human concepts and descriptions. The agnostic's experience of the Incomprehensible and the Ineffable is a negative one. It is negative in the sense that in all of it the only thing that can be formulated is what one does *not* experience and does *not* know. The Real escapes us totally. But can we even speak of "totally"? Is there no listening to the zone of silence? Is there no gazing in the direction of the Invisible, even though one cannot enter this zone nor "grasp" the numinous? "I cannot say what cannot be said, but sounds make us listen to the silence."[4] The word "silence" carries a twofold meaning in this context: it is that which does not make itself knowable to us, that which does not reveal itself, but most of all it is that for which we can find no words and for which we can only stand dumb with amazement. This experience is not so far removed from what Christian tradition has always called "negative theology," a theology which can only tell us who God is *not,* because he transcends and breaks through all human concepts. In the words of Pseudo-Dionysius the Areopagite: "With relation to the divine, unknowings are true; affirmations, however, are always insufficient." The reflective person in fact knows better what God certainly is *not* than who he *is* in essence. God is *not* good in the way we commonly refer to "being good." God is *not* powerful in the sense normally given to the term "power." God does not know love, at least not the sort of love we usually mean when they use that word.

If the Mysterious is experienced as that about which nothing adequate can be said, does this mean at the same time that there can nowhere be found an interpretative echo of this sort of experience? Cannot a poet draw our attention to the Unnameable in such a way that we begin to listen to its Silence? Certainly language cannot say what cannot be said, but language can indeed say *why* it cannot say certain things. Language can say that there is a Reality which transcends all adequate speech. In his poem "Carnac," Guillevic speaks of the sea which hammers against the Breton rocks without, however, breaking through them. In this sea, he sees humankind never breaking through the way of Mystery but still holding to the notion that there could be "Something" behind the wall about which "nothing" exact is known. Here the wall is not transcended. Still, it is more the beginning of the Invisible than the end of the Real. In the use of this image of a wall, not everything is said, even though it is difficult to say any more. For the agnostic Guillevic, his feeling of constriction became the stimulus for suspicions regarding the existence of more spacious though impenetrable regions. In his "Dialogue with the Sea," Guillevic sees how the ocean, precisely like humankind, is moved up and down by a higher power or law which escapes understanding. Like the sea, humanity experiences insuperable rocky shores or frontiers on the one hand, and an invisible, transcendent regularity on the other. To say

something about this Invisible is impossible for him: "That
which cannot be said." But, as if in dialogue with himself, the
poet says to the visible sea:

> You come and you go
> But within limits
> Fixed by a law
> Which is not from you.
> We have in common
> The experience of the wall. (13)

> Wall which is perhaps only made
> Of absence
> Of reply to question.
> So, enter
> Into an absence, then? (17)

> These margins . . . are the center
> Of what is not directly said,
> Can't be, shouldn't be said
> Except in speaking
> Of what is round about.
> There is respect. (18)[5]

Guillevic's admission (in stanza 18) is striking: that one can
indeed say something *indirectly* about the invisible center, namely by speaking about that which lies *around* the center. Hence, we
can gather some idea of the Invisible by way of the visible only
when the latter becomes transparent. We can only say something meaningful about the "other side" by speaking about this
side: the "earthly," in fact, is continually smashing against the
wall of Mystery. So, the "earthly" reaches Mystery and thereby
comes into contact with it. Here we are strikingly close to the
Christian affirmation that God always reveals himself "mediate-

ly," i.e., through what Tillich called "Offenbarungsträger" (bearers of revelation) or media. God can reveal himself in nature (i.e., in his creation), through history (i.e., through that which he lets his people experience in a "salvation history" or through the things he lets happen providentially, not accidentally, to an individual person) and especially through the God-man Christ, the divine symbol par excellence.[6] That such an indirect revelation of the Transcendent is possible, or at least conceivable, Guillevic affirms in the final stanza:

> If there was a place
> Which would finally open
> To the one who steps forward
> To see what is happening
> At the last precipice . . .
> Where, as a prize for courage,
> Everything would be given him,
> Who would not go to the sacrifice?" (23)

Who would not be prepared to sacrifice all that is visible for the vision of the Invisible when it would finally be revealed? Meanwhile, Guillevic's position here is the typical religious attitude of surprised and admiring veneration. The agnostic prefers to keep quiet about what might or might not be transcendent because nothing certain is known about it. "If we should not know, if there is nothing to know, then why this desire to know?"[7]

2. The "Natural" Experience of Transcendence

The "natural" experience of transcendence, or, in its purest form, "natural mysticism," is a non-supernatural "peak experience" capable of being explained by psychology. Psychological methods of concentration, the practice of yoga, drugs, techniques of meditation, slow repetition over and over again of a certain word, calm gazing with bowed head at one's navel (cf.

Greek *hesychasm*), recourse to dance and music, and watching handsome young lads as certain Sufi "ascetics" practiced are only a few of the many means employed by people of various cultures, occasionally with a fair amount of success, for arousing and cultivating such "peak experiences."[8] Although phenomenological descriptions of these experiences often borrow religious jargon, still the real attention is never on the "wholly Other" but rather on the spectacular side of *one's own* experience. These experiences are never seen as the result of the approach of God, but rather of the efforts and natural talent of the person engaging in the exercise. The "I" is not rejoicing over an encounter with a "Thou," but over its *own* expansion of consciousness. It is not God that is sought, let alone found, but devotion. The concern is not for the beloved but with one's own spiritual eroticism. It is still the "amabam amare" (I love to be in love) of the young Augustine, not yet his "amo Deum" (I love God).

What exactly is experienced in such natural "peak experiences"? Ordinary sense perception and discursive thought are suddenly transcended by a remarkable realization of unity. Everything becomes "relative" in the light of this contemplation of unity. The person in question has the impression of only *now* experiencing genuine reality compared to which everything else pales. Not only Jung and Huxley but even Ruusbroec was convinced that such experiences exist and are able to be explained psychologically. Hence, they lie unquestionable *within* the possibilities of human nature.

For Jung, they are experiences of a manic or hallucinatory sort. That which for the neurotic is a "belch" from an overly repressed collective unconscious is for the ascetic the long-awaited awakening of what is deepest in the human psyche, that for which the ascetic has finally learned to make room by directing his or her attention away from what is unimportant. In both cases it has to do with an effervescence of the irrational, unconscious part of the soul that overflows into the reason which is so one-sidedly privileged in the West. It is not God that is experienced here but a still conscious aspect of my "ego": namely, my archetype "God."

So here it is not a question of the experience of God but rather a new "self-consciousness," a peak in the flat, even landscape of everyday human experience. But there are no Olympian gods living on this peak. It is only the highest point (or the deepest level) of the human psyche. Most people never reach it, and in our days never even suspect its existence. But when I am atop Mont Blanc, I am still in French territory, not in heaven, even though reaching the mountaintop gives the climber a "heavenly feeling." It is characteristic of this sort of ecstatic experience that it brings with it no consequences for the moral, active life. Both good and evil people through training or effort can experience such a thing. They stay just as good or evil as they ever were. This is the reason why Ruusbroec was so highly critical of "natural mysticism." For him, this psychological state of consciousness has nothing to do with faith or religion. It is an experience theoretically available to anyone, given certain psychological, profane techniques.

How does Ruusbroec describe such an experience? "When (a person) is denuded of all sense representations, and empty and inactive as far as discursive thought is concerned, then he arrives at an interior rest in a purely natural way. Anyone can arrive at such a rest in his deepest center, and continue in this state in a purely natural manner, without the grace of God, if only he can empty himself of all representations and activities." How does a person reach such a state? "Behold, this is the way in which a person cultivates this natural rest. It is an immobility, without any interior or exterior busy-ness, so that this rest can be, first, discovered, and, then, preserved undisturbed."[9] Hence a condition is reached that is remarkably close to what Buddhism calls "Nirvana," a quieting of all sense perception and imagination, of all thought, of all attention which one could give to any form of desire or longing. It is a condition of blessed emptiness and psychological rest. In the words of a classical Buddhist: "The withdrawal from, turning away from, absence of, all passion; emptiness, rest, higher knowledge, enlightenment, in a word, Nirvana."[10]

For Ruusbroec, the reason why such a condition has nothing in common with relationship to God lies in the fact that neither love of God nor charity for one's neighbor is strengthened by it. Rather, the contrary is true. Here one's whole attention is riveted on a noble feeling of the self, of which the deeper dimensions are now being experienced. What one discovers is the "true self" but not a relationship with the Transcendent. Rather, attention is turned away from what, for the Christian, is essential: God.

What is more, the experience is not followed by nobler deeds, and this is Ruusbroec's second criticism of it. It does not lead to an elevated sense of morality. It is a magnificent tree, but devoid of fruit. Worse yet, in this state of quietism, the ecstatic, as a rule, has a sense of having been raised above rules and obligations. "For according to their own imagination, they have outgrown all practices and moral obligations. . . . They claim to be free and thus elevated above all God's commandments, above the law and above every form of the practice of virtue."

But there is still more. The cultivation of a "natural" experience of transcendence is not only an occasion to neglect one's obligations to be committed to other human beings, but Ruusbroec also sees in it the danger of pride, spiritual gluttony and "unchastity"—first of all pride, since here it is a question of an exceptional state, that is, an extraordinary, non-everyday experience which, in spite of its theoretical possibility for everyone, is nonetheless not reserved for all.

Since the experience is sought on account of the experience itself, like eating for the delicious taste and not for nourishment, we can certainly speak of "spiritual gluttony" here. What is sought is "consolation, sweetness, enjoyment, internal savor and the spiritual pleasure of human nature," according to Ruusbroec. The danger then lies in the fact that one remains so busy with one's own tasting and savoring, with the expansion of one's own world of experience, that the essentials, other people, the world, and God, escape notice.

Finally, Ruusbroec ventures to speak of "spiritual unchastity" or self-gratification. "Spiritual unchastity is the disordered inclination of natural love when it always falls back upon itself and seeks only its own pleasure in everything. . . . Such a natural love remains bent upon itself and concentrated upon its own enjoyment; in so doing, it always remains alone."[11] Just as "unchaste love" shows some resemblance to married love while in reality it is only a travesty and betrayal of it, so also ecstasy that has been psychologically aroused *resembles* love for God, though in essence it has nothing to do with it, according to Ruusbroec. Nothing so strikingly resembles an original painting as a reproduction of it. But a reproduction is not a painting.

The extremely reserved attitude taken by Ruusbroec toward the "way of natural light" is very timely for us since today a considerable amount of literature on experiences of transcendence, having no connection with anything ecclesiastical, moral, or specifically religious, is finding a steadily growing dissemination. Psychological experiences of this genre are not evil. No use of natural talent should be called evil. The danger is only that one might think that it is a question of "religious experience" here, or, what would be worse, that genuine religious experience about which we will speak at greater length later could likewise be reduced to nothing but a simple psychological process. Then "God" would be nothing more than a certain deeper dimension of my psychology. Those who have that idea "do not know what they are missing," according to Ruusbroec. Those who confuse God with the mysterious depths of their unconscious ego do not know what they are lacking. Only a careful description of the phenomenological distinction between the various sorts of transcendental experiences and of their use of language can bring to light the real distinctions which there are between them.

The testimony of the French novelist Marcel Proust is valuable in this respect. Because of his Catholic education, religious jargon was not foreign to him. Yet not for a second does it occur to him that in his natural ecstasy there is anything "religious" to be seen. He lucidly put his experiences into words, using purely profane concepts. In fact, as far as he is concerned, these are unforgettable, psychological peak moments. He sees no more in them than that. "No sooner had the warm liquid, and . . . the (cake-) crumbs with it, touched my palate than a shudder ran through my whole body, and I stopped, intent upon the *extraordinary* changes that were taking place. An exquisite pleasure had invaded my senses, but individual, detached, with no suggestion of its origin. And at once the vicissitudes of life had become indifferent to me, its disasters innocuous, *its brevity illusory*—this new sensation having had on me the effect which love has of filling me with a precious essence; or rather this essence was not in me, it *was* myself. I had ceased now to feel *mediocre, accidental, mortal.*"[12]

It is not God which is experienced here but the "eternal I" hidden behind the banal, historical, everyday "I." If this "eternal I" becomes conscious for some at times, it is only then that it becomes clear to them how futile the transitory world is and why only the timeless and eternal can have value. My deeper "I" makes me realize that I do not need to be apprehensive of death, of the future, of illness or misfortune. I am eternal on the deepest level of my thoughts. I transcend time. It is a question of moments sometimes called "metapsychological" or "peak-experiences." Such moments are so overpowering that someone like Proust "almost loses consciousness" in them. Finally, Proust's testimony is interesting because his experience is so close to the

Buddhist ideal: behind the transitoriness of the historical "I" a "real being" is experienced which is "unborn and uncreated, subject to no process of becoming, and which shall never undergo disintegration." We look in vain for concepts such as creation, salvation *history* or love life in such descriptions. We are dealing with psychology and not theology, self-consciousness and not experience of God.

3. *"Pan-en-henism" of the Disappearance of the Self into the All*

The term "Pan-en-henism" (everything is one, and that One, in fact, embraces everything) is to be preferred to the more usual term "Pantheism" (everything is God) because, in the experience of transcendence about which we are speaking here, nothing is said about God as such. But what is at issue here is rather an ecstatic realization that I as a human being am indeed transitory, but nature, or the Cosmos, is eternal, and that these latter will take me up eventually into their all-embracing greatness. The human person, as self-consciousness or as center of experiences and activities, disappears and is absorbed into the Universal. This Universal is eternal. But it is not regarded as a person, a God. It is not a theistic but a monistic experience, that is, there is no notion of God but rather an idea of unity that transcends all transitoriness or historicity. The core of this experience is that Reality is eternal, while I as person am transitory and shall have to disappear into the Eternal. A person drowns in the shoreless sea of the Transcendent. These devout people think that men and women, while here on earth, only long for a dreamless sleep in eternal rest within the bosom of the All. Hence we have the death-wish and the Nirvana-principle of Freud. With that, we are back in the clutches of psychology.

Anyone who ever visited the meditation garden in a Buddhist monastery can attest that such a "garden," which is always the image of the cosmos or the "All," contains only stones and rocks, harmoniously disposed over weedless gravel. If a plant or little tree is found here or there, then it is placed there in such a way that all growth and change seem excluded. The plants are kept "small," i.e., unchangeable, as much as possible. This horticultural material for meditation is supposed to bring visitors to the notion of their own littleness and "nothingness" in the literal sense of the word as compared to the unchangeable, eternal cosmos. Someone who meditates in this way sees in nature not the traces of a creating God, but the timeless rest of unity in which the futile self must gradually disappear if it is to find salvation and peace.

Does not classical Chinese painting betray the selfsame spirituality? A minuscule figure of a person walks, almost lost, in the wealth of superabundant nature. Nature, far from serving as the background for the portrait of a central human figure, is the real theme in Chinese art. The tiny person gets lost therein, or wanders about, forlorn. Some Westerners, even those with a Christian background, have also known this sort of experience naturally. William James cites the testimony of two men who, under the impression of an enthralling natural experience, passed over from a conscious relationship with God to "pan-en-henism." The first asserts: "I never lost the consciousness of the presence of God until I stood at the foot of the Horseshoe Falls, Niagara. Then I lost him in the immensity of what I saw. I also lost myself, feeling that I was an atom too small for the notice of almighty God." The second testimonial is still more exact, if possible: "A presence, I might say, yet that is too suggestive of personality, and the moments of which I speak did not hold the consciousness of a personality, but something in myself made me feel myself a part of something bigger than I, that was controlling. I felt myself one with the grass, the trees, birds, insects, everything in nature."[13] The central thing is always the loss of personality, which nevertheless is not experienced as extinction but as the only real life. Consciousness of my individuality appears to dissolve and gradually to pass over into a boundless existence.

In connection with this, the spiritual evolution of Rimbaud ("a mystic in the wild state," as Claudel called him) is worthy of note. Rimbaud was familiar with Christianity. His religious hunger was real, though it was perhaps more a question of hunger for experience than longing for God. "Greedily I await God," wrote the young poet. But such an experience did not come. Like a spoiled child, the poet begins to chide God for this with curses and complaints. When God does not react in a sensibly perceptible way either to the wild provocations or to immature prayers, Rimbaud capriciously turns his back upon him. This young man looking for God, tired out and disillusioned by his whims, now becomes an "a-theistic" hunter for transcendence. Out of his frustrated rebelliousness, he henceforth seeks his salvation in the repose of impersonal pan-en-henism. "I returned to the Orient and to the first and eternal wisdom," he writes. In fact, he dreams of an ascent into nature without the mature obligation of action or commitment, without responsibility or morality, only enjoying spiritual rest. In a word what awakens in him is what Freud and Rank would call an "immature desire for a return to the security of the womb."

However, the repose of pan-en-henism, clearly a last resort for Rimbaud, would eventually depart from him. The realization that God *is* there, in spite of everything, remained too clearly within him. Rimbaud *knew* that his quietistic search for Eastern, psychological repose was an illusion. "At last, I shall ask forgiveness for having fed on lies," he cries out, after having ascertained that instead of the long-awaited paradise, that is, instead of a regressive "limbo-innocence," his whole experience had been a "season in hell." And the unfortunate man looking for God concluded despondently: "Spiritual combat is as brutal as the battle of men; but the vision of justice is the pleasure of God alone."[14]

4. *Ascetical Isolation of "the True Self"*

Even more so than Christian and Moslem spiritual masters, Indian spiritual leaders attribute great importance to "detachment." For an Indian guru, one must gradually free oneself from all that can disturb "the spiritual" within. If Christians and Moslems practice detachment in order to more totally attach themselves to God, among Indians its goal is the discovery of the core of one's "true self." Here, God is not the partner whom I love. The Indian rather sees God as did the Netherlands poet Kloos: "I am a god in the deepest part of my thoughts." Indian gods are paths leading to the eternal, timeless Self. By concentrating in meditation on one or another divinity, I "forget" all the futility and transitoriness to which I am so attached by nature, in order to seek the only Reality: "the soul of all that lives." At the same time, the "soul of the All" is my own soul. As a matter of fact, here, too, the adage is true that "all is One." For the Indian, that "One" is purely spiritual. Matter, or nature, on the other hand, is pure illusion from which a person has to become detached.

The difference from the Christian view of things is clear. For the Christian, the deepest level of the human soul, sometimes called "the apex or point of the soul" by Christian mystics, is the place where God dwells in the human person. This, therefore, is the place where the mystic encounters and experiences God. For the Indian, on the other hand, this psychic level is identical with God. The soul, thus, is not the place where God binds himself to us in love; the soul *is* God. Here Oriental monism stands in contrast to the Christian experience of relationship. For the Hindu, there is basically only one Reality: God. This God is nothing more than the center of my true "self." Everything else is an unimportant world of appearances. Only one who is fully detached from the illusory snares of the phenomenal world, in other words, from whatever our material senses can perceive and enjoy here on earth, is capable of discovering his or her "true self."

This is the reason why an ascetical technique such as yoga is so important in the life of the convinced Hindu. Yoga is the road to the gradual redemption from the corporeal. The consequence of this spiritual attitude is a striking depreciation of matter and of any concrete commitment within this transitory world. Of lesser importance for the Hindu are politics, charitable institutions, technical progress, physics (in contrast with metaphysics), etc. Teilhard de Chardin, devoted to God's created matter in a typically Christian way, has also lamented this Oriental one-sidedness: "India allowed itself to be drawn into metaphysics, only to become lost there. . . . These (mystical) currents, with their excessive passivity and detachment, were incapable of building the world."

If the final end of the Christian religious ascent is an intense experience of happiness and of love (the "beatific vision"), the Indian's Omega point is just the opposite: the *cessation* of all experiences. When the transitory, historical, psychological "I" is ultimately melted away into the One, there *is* nothing more that can be perceived or experienced by this One. The One, then, as a Subject, no longer has any object before it. Therefore, eternity is not the experience of happiness: eternity is the *elimination* of any experience. Eternity is a state of perfect, passionless rest, a single, infinite sea, which washes up on no more shores, for there *are* no more shores or frontiers. Outside of the immense "Sea," there *is* nothing else. Everything is swallowed up into it and disappears. There is not even anyone left to see this sea, to love it, or to contemplate it in ecstasy.

Nevertheless, the greatest of the Indian mystics have broken through this pantheistic monism numerous times, entering into a genuine I-Thou relationship between the human person and God in much the same way that Christians experience it. As a matter of fact, the Bhagavad-Gita, often called the "Hindu Bible," contains several "theistic" passages, passages in which the worshiper addresses God as a "Thou." This book marked a genuine turning point for Hindu spirituality. Identity between the human soul and God is ultimately given up. In place of pantheism, an authentic monotheism makes its appearance. Henceforth, *love* of God for humans and a consequent human love for God, the central givens of the Jewish-Christian revelation, are spoken of within Hinduism.

The last chapter of the Bhagavad-Gita uses language that sounds almost Christian to cast light upon this reciprocal love between God and human beings, a love which is pure grace or gift of God. Here we are immediately far removed from ascetical concentration on one's own "Self." The world is no longer evil. The material world is God's creation and therefore points to God, although it can also keep God concealed, in particular from those who shortsightedly cling to what is worldly.

The incarnated god Krishna, therefore, says to his disciple Arjuna: "Freed from egotism, force, arrogance, desire, anger and possession (an ascetical beginning, countering all privately-owned possessions apart from God), the true lover never refuses the partner anything: unselfish, peaceful, he is fit to become Brahman (his true essence). Having become Brahman, tranquil in the Self, he neither grieves nor desires (something a Christian could not say: for, on the one hand, he *feels* the cross, and, on the other, his love *longs* more and more for its Partner). Regarding all beings as equal, he attains supreme devotion to me. (Hence, religious love is grace. It is received. Monism is broken through, for to love, there have to be at least two beings.) By devotion he *knows* me, what my measure is and what I am essentially. (Hence there is an experience of God, a 'knowledge' that seems possible only in love and in faith.) Then having known me essentially, he *enters forthwith into me.* (In other words, unity is achieved without connecting links such as nature, sacraments, ritual, charitable love for one's fellow man, etc. The mystic experiences God 'without intermediary.') Here again my supreme word, the most secret of all: thou art greatly beloved by me; hence I will speak for thy good. Center thy mind on me, be devoted to me, sacrifice to me, revere me, and thou shalt come to me. I promise thee truly, for thou art dear to me."[16]

Such peak-experiences of a love-relationship with God are not all that infrequent in Hinduism. Ramakrishna, in the nineteenth century, extends love for God to love for neighbor. Here he comes remarkably close to the Gospel message of neighborly love. "Perfect knowledge is attained only when God is recognized in man. Now I see that he it is who is found among us under so many forms: now as an honorable person, then again as a fraud or a scoundrel."[17] This is not far from Christ's word that what one does for the least of his brethren, particularly sinners, one does for him.

This Hindu mystic never wrote a word himself. Nevertheless, he lies at the root of an important religious renewal in India. In India, principally through his most famous disciple Vivekananda, he made Hinduism more and more known, even in the West. Officially, Ramakrishna drew from the monistic-pantheistic Vedanta philosophy. But in his personal experiential life, he clearly appears to have been a pious devotee of a personal God whose creation was an act of love. As with many other non-Christian mystics, we find here a split between two, basically irreconcilable, views. On the theoretical level, he affirms an "orthodox" teaching of monistic integration into the eternal All, but on the practical level (i.e., in the order of experience) he describes a personal love-experience between the soul and God (Kali). It was his doctrine of creation, which contains scarcely any differences from the creation-concept of Christianity, that rectified the theoretical pantheism of this mystic. In fact, R. C. Zaehner notes: "In the Bhagavad-Gita God slowly *disengages* himself from the universe (hence, no longer an *integration,* but a first step toward *duality* of relationship between Creator and creature) of which he is still the material as well as the efficient cause, and confronts man as Person to person. The Bhagavad-Gita is thus the watershed that separates the pantheistic monism of the Upanishads (texts which constitute the basis of the Vedanta philosophy to which Ramakrishna officially adhered) from the fervent theism (relationship with a God or with diverse popular incarnations of the divinity) of the later popular cults (found scattered all over India)."[18]

Practically all the utterances of Ramakrishna that were written down and that stimulated much of the growing Western interest in Hinduism are wholly within the scope of this theistic Bhagavad-Gita spirituality. The Hinduism of Ramakrishna or of Gandhi deals with a *personal* God who loves his human creatures no matter to what caste they may belong. This sort of Hinduism is already preaching far less about the ascetical isolation of one's "true self."

Finally, let us note that texts in which Oriental monism is broken through and in which God is experienced as Someone or Something with whom (or with which) the human person enters into relationship are also sometimes found within Zen Buddhism. Testimonials such as the following are certainly not isolated examples in Buddhist mysticism: "The state of objectlessness is not the final one (i.e., in which all created objects disappear and are absorbed into the eternal All). An ancient master warns us not to mistake the state of unconsciousness or objectlessness for the truth. While in this state, however, you happen to hear a sound or to perceive an object, and then, all of a sudden, the whole thing bursts upon you, you have at last touched the ultimate Reality."[19] The ultimate phase in transcendental experience therefore is no longer "the cessation of all personal experience in Nirvana," for it is not true that there would be no other objects outside myself. For that matter, I do not disappear into the All. Here, the highest religious experience is a "contact" with Something which was occasionally

heard or experienced previously, but which now suddenly reveals itself to me in an illumination. I gaze at this "something"
in a state of utter astonishment and of contemplation: "And in
the illuminating moment everything stands open to its gaze (i.e.,
of the human spirit)."

With testimonials such as these, we have finally arrived at
the fifth form of transcendental experience: the theistic experience of a love-relationship between the human person and God.
Hence, the experience of "re-ligio" in the strict sense of the
word: the continual being-bound-back to God.

5. The "Religious" Love-Relationship Between God and Humanity

Jews, Moslems, and Christians are in agreement that they
see the relationship of humans with God as a love-relationship.
Anyone who speaks of love immediately thinks of concepts such
as uniting, becoming one, or unity. No matter how far one might
progress along the way of the unification process, no matter
how interior the love bond may gradually become, in order to
experience love, there must always be, and remain, *two* partners.
Here religion is seen as a bond, not as a fusion, a relationship
between partners, not as an identification. The human droplet
never disappears into the divine sea. God has willed and created
human beings with his personal selfhood. It is precisely on account of this selfhood that God continues to love his child eternally.

If Judaism and Islam, with the exception of their greatest
mystics, emphasize the unbridgeable chasm between the transcendent God and puny human beings, the culminating point
for Christianity is God's "incarnation" as bridge from the Divine
to the human. God comes to us in such a radical way that he
even goes to the length of taking on an historical condition. In
Christ, God becomes human. But, we repeat, God does not dis-

appear here, nor is he absorbed in pure humanity, as Feuerbach figured. In other words, God is not a human projection. Since Christ, God lives *in* human form; he dwells in the human. The highest that a person on earth can achieve is mystical "unity" in "rest" (Ruusbroec), resting and lying almost lost in the arms of the Divine Partner. And yet, we do not thereby lose our human selfhood. We *remain* finite, full of desires forever, no matter how divinized we become by being taken up in the Holy Trinity's interplay of love. In order to be able to experience, contemplate and enjoy God in eternity, we must remain a partner; hence, "not-God," but human. The uniqueness of this Christian experience of God will be explained further in the following chapter.

· 6 ·

The Uniqueness of
the Christian Experience
of God

1. *God Is a Person*

Moltmann contends that "the I-Thou relationship is the model of relationship with God."[1] It would perhaps be more exact to say that the "I-Thou" relationship is the typical Judaeo-Christian form of relationship with God. Non-Christians may see in God the absolute Ground of their being, the universal All, eternal Being, or the "One." Jew and Christian, and the Moslem after them, however, experience God as a living person who reveals himself and comes to us, who helps, punishes, redeems or concludes a covenant with human beings. The destiny of his human creatures does not leave God cold. Hölderlin is speaking more of the Greek gods than of the Christian God of revelation when he affirms:

The gods live, it is true,
But in another world, up above,

They work on endlessly there and seem to take little
    notice
Whether we live, so much do the celestials care for us!

Seen in Christian perspective, God does *not* live "in another
world." "The kingdom of God is in the midst of you" (Lk
17:21). God does pay attention to whether and how we live. It
directly concerns him. The God-human relationship is a "dia-
logical" relationship. What a person says in prayer "touches"
God. Sooner or later we may expect a reply or reaction. That
"reply," then, will in turn incite us to express gratitude, or lead
us possibly to a still more urgent request. Inversely, as Christians we know that God can "call" us to a task. Then, in turn,
God waits for an actual reply on our part. God's further dealings
with us depend upon the reply we give.

Hence, there is a story, a true "love story," between God
and human beings. The story is different for each one of us
since we answer, or fail to answer, God's invitation in our own
way. A Christian never ascribes what happens to him or her to
blind fate but to God's providence. God knows this; God wills
this, or at least permits it. God can turn it all to good. If a person
does not understand things that happen and are willed by God,
who is benevolent and almighty, then that person prays with
Paul: "How inscrutable are thy judgments, how unsearchable
thy ways" (Rom 11:33). A Christian does not adopt this astonishing attitude in response to negligence or to lovelessness on
the part of God, but on the contrary accepts the fact that God
has more insight than any human. In a word, the believer ac-
knowledges the "depths of the riches and wisdom and knowledge of God" (Rom 11:33).

The Christian also does not see world events as products of
an accidental chain-reaction of blind cause and effect, possibly
set in motion by a "first Mover." The believer sees a meaning in
history, as well as in whatever befalls each person in particular.

"In everything God works for good with those who love him" (Rom 8:28). Ultimately God brings the believer to the "Omega point" or to the "reign of God." True, the way along which God calls us moves through various historical and unexpected circumstances. In the Bible we find the repercussion of God's saving deeds on his Jewish people (Old Testament) and on his Church (New Testament). On the other hand, it is in the testimonies of mystics throughout the history of the Church that we find descriptions of the ways in which God has loved a specific individual and gradually drawn that person to himself. It is clear that here we are speaking in anthropomorphic terms. Religious language is always analogous language. It makes use of concepts distilled from sense perception and projects these on God, to speak figuratively. Since God can never be perceived by any of our senses, we must speak of him in an indirect, symbolic way. Whatever is experienced *directly* with God can only be put into words *indirectly*, using comparisons or analogies. In Christian perspective, what a person experiences with God resembles most what can be experienced with other human beings. This reveals the great difficulty of believing in God when one person does not yet know how to believe in another. It also shows the problem of loving God when a person has not so much as had the chance to experience human love. As a Christian, I experience God as Someone whom I love, because I know that I am so much loved by him. God is Someone who understands me, listens to me, and enters into dialogue with me. Certainly, we are not dealing here with "just" a comparison: the reality is much more marvelous. But I cannot express it better than with concepts of human love. There is no other human experience closer to what a person experiences with God than the bond of erotic love between persons. Hence a Christian regards God more as a "person" than as "Ground of Being," "First Mover," "The All" or any other abstract reality.

Moreover the Christian experiences God as a Person, not as

an Idea. Philosophically there are two notions of "person" in circulation in the West. The first is of pagan origin and came from Aristotle via Boethius to Thomas Aquinas. Here, person is "an individual substance (a being standing by itself) endowed with rational nature," and the emphasis is upon independence. The second, less widespread notion stems directly from Christian mysticism. Here the emphasis is upon relationship. When the mystic, Richard of St. Victor, describes the Trinity as a "love-life of three Persons," what exactly does he mean by "Persons"? It has to do with something which originally became real for him not in the people he met but in the Trinitarian God he experienced. What does Christian mysticism understand by a trinitarian Person? Person is a loving orientation toward others. "Person" means essentially "standing in relationship," an ex- sistentia, an "esse ad alios." It is the love which one experiences, which one gives and receives, that constitutes the person. "The true self is always brought into being by love."[2] Person is essen- tially "inclination," i.e., someone who is altogether bent and bowed toward the other. The "divine Persons" are such, at any rate. We are now called to construct and experience our own person in that same way, although imperfectly and analogously to be sure. The human person is created after God's image and likeness in order to love. Being human is a call to become more and more "personal" in relationship with others. In other words, the human person is created gradually to *become* human in the fullest sense of the word.

The Christian mystic does not experience God as a lonely, monolithic Allah. For him, God is essentially love. If there were only *one* Person in God, then it would be hard to say that God was "love" before creation existed. Love stands in need of oth- ers. But before the creation, there were no others apart from God, no one who could be known or experienced or loved by God, no one with whom God could share himself or from whom he could receive love in return. The Christian knows that the Father sees and loves the Son from all eternity. "Supposing that there existed but one Person in the divinity, then this one would have no one with whom he could share the riches of his majesty. And, on the other hand, he would necessarily be eternally deprived of the abundance of delight and sweetness with which an intimate love could have enriched him."[3]

A person is not an island or a fixed substance which happens to be capable of building accidental bridges out to "another" who might arrive on the scene. It is the bridge of relationship which constitutes a person. To put it even more forcefully, person *is* relationship. A child becomes a person by being spoken to and loved by its mother. Self-consciousness is awakened in conversation with another. First comes language, and then, and only then, subjectivity. First, I speak, and thereby I become myself: a person. "Discourse provokes emergence of subjectivity," says Benveniste. Self-consciousness or the notion that I am a person is always a reflection of my speaking with a "thou." "It is in and through language that the person is constituted as subject, for it is language alone which bases the concept of 'go' in reality. I use 'I' uniquely in addressing myself to someone who will be a 'thou' for me."[4]

We say of God that he is a Person because divine life, seen as Trinity, is essentially intersubjective communication. God is love relationship. First of all, this is true among the three Persons mutually. Moreover, the Father loves and sees in the Son his creature, the human person, whose ultimate vocation it is to be taken up within this Trinitarian love experience. It is of this Trinitarian love experience that the Christian mystic has knowledge. It is in his or her experience of God that the mystic begins to realize what it really means to be a person. This is why we are right in calling the mystical understanding of person more "theomorphic" than "anthropomorphic." It grows out of contemplation of God and not out of looking at other human beings. It is born of mysticism and not of psychology. The "personal" life to which everyone is called is only an "image and likeness" or an analogy of that which the Trinitarian God is to the fullest extent from all eternity. Hence, we can say that where there is intentionality (i.e., desire directed toward a "thou"), where there is hospitality, where I accord the other a place in my attention and in my heart, then there is subjectivity or personness in the basic sense of the word. This is always true for God in an eminent way. In an analogous, imperfect way, each human will try to take a "personal" stance with regard to God and fellow humans. Each will try to seek "contact" and, if possible, a lasting relationship. Each will try to become a "personality."

In connection with this, a distinction is often made between *person* and *personality*. Person then means dynamism, the primary desire for others with which everyone is born. The person seeks affection and also wants to be able to give it to others. A personality, on the other hand, is a piece of mature history. Personality is what a person has accomplished in life up to now, an historical, steadily-developed network of relationships of varying profundity. Hence, personality refers to a product of one's history. It is a concrete human face upon which one's lot in life, one's experiences of disappointments and of happiness with others, with the world and with God, have left their traces. Personality is a drama or a novel of which the "person" is at one and the same time both author and main character. It is a novel that is not finished as long as that person is still alive.[5]

It always remains possible for a person to build up new relationships, to deepen existing ones, or, inversely, to let them get bogged down. Whether a personality is balanced, lonely, or neurotic depends on the type, the depth, and the complexity of the relationships which have made it little by little into what it has become.

In addition to this Christian concept of person, sprung from mysticism, we find a second, more widespread definition of what a person is. Although of pagan origin, this second concept has nevertheless found many adherents within Christian philosophy and even theology. There, "person" is understood as an individual who is spiritually endowed by existing independently. As Boethius expressed it: "Rationalis naturae individua substantia" (individual substance of rational nature). Abelard, Richard of St. Victor, and St. Thomas had already seen that God could not be called "person" in this sense of the word. In fact, God is not a "being standing by itself." He is not a specific being, not an object, not a thing, not a being in addition to other beings. God is essentially relationship, a love relationship at that. If Ionesco was correct when he observed that "atheism is often a misunderstanding of language," then it can certainly be said that a confusion of ideas with reference to God's "person-ness" can be called the cause of many of today's faith problems and modern agnosticism. When a Christian claims to have experienced God, he or she is not claiming to have met an "essence" living somewhere in spiritual solitude. Rather, Christian experience of God is the realization that I find myself, in spite of everything, in the secure hands of Someone who loves me. It is the idea of relationship, not of a thing. It is an experience of love, not of an existence standing outside of or in addition to me. Another human being is not an "objective entity," either. A person is someone whom I love or fear, or who leaves me indifferent. "My 'other' is defined solely by the suffering or the pleasure that he gives me."[6]

If as often happens I treat another human as a thing, then I am acting inhumanly and am thereby immoral. Since God and humans can be so intimately related with each other, it is not surprising that for the medieval mind and until the sixteenth century anthropology was not yet cut off from theology. People did not yet make an "abstraction" of God in order to examine the human partner as though that half of the relationship were a minuscule island. Nature and supernature were not yet separated. The "supernatural" relationship with God was still seen as belonging to the very nature, or essence, of being human. The human person was created with an aching desire for God ("Thou has made us for thyself, O Lord"). The medieval craving after God, something which in modern times has to a great extent become unconscious, was not an "accidental circumstance" of which one could make abstraction on the so-called "purely human" level. Reflection on the human phenomenon (anthropology) meant at the same time meditating about God (theology).

For the great Reformers Luther and Calvin, anthropology and theology were still not two separate sciences. On the other hand, they were just that for their Catholic opponents of the Renaissance. When Luther and the Dominican Cajetan countered each other in 1517, unable to come to reconciliation, it was not basically a theological dispute. If the difference in meaning had been of a theological nature, then Protestants and Catholics could still have avoided the rupture. Within the Catholic camp itself, theological disputes had existed for a long time. We have only to recall the fierce battles between Dominicans and Jesuits on this score. But the really disintegrating influence was the totally divergent views about the nature of being human. Luther and Calvin saw human beings, albeit severely damaged by sin, as beings joined by nature to God, a typically religious medieval way of thinking. Cajetan, and with him all Renaissance theologians, had a "humanistic" view of the human condition. He left "nature" to "anthropologists," in this instance, "philosophers." "Supernature" was his area of expertise as a theologian. The opposing sides in 1517 were made up of, on the one side, a "vertical anthropology," and, on the other, a theology of the supernatural.

The struggle between Catholics and Protestants was aggravated during a typical cultural crisis or transition period, namely, while the entire scientific climate of thought was changing. This explains the difficulty that moderns have in grasping what was really going on in this conflict which had so many long-term consequences. Today's Christians are much more quickly inclined to throw the cloak of ecumenical toleration over their historic understanding. It was not so much *what* people thought about God and humans which differed. The pinch came in the *manner in which* they theologized. The dispute was not dogmatic, but methodological. There were no divergent understandings about the being of God, but rather about the knowledge of human beings.

Luther was not thinking like a professional theologian accompanied by specialized philosophers and anthropologists. For him the human sciences had not yet developed into a broad spectrum in which theology would appear as a separate, well-defined, independent area of expertise. When Luther spoke of the human person, his description was simultaneously colored by philosophy, psychology, and theology. For example, we have only to think of his concretely phenomenological and biblical manner of speaking when he discussed "human faith." That was indeed the way people thought in the Middle Ages. Theorizing about the human condition from a "purely anthropological" point of view, and hence apart from biblical revelation, was a foreign idea. For the medieval thinker, "natural" humanity was an unreal, even sinful, abstraction, which current methodological considerations could not allow. The "grace" of a Christian's relationship with God was not a supernatural superstructure, nor was it a meta-anthropological addendum that was the exclusive territory of specialized professional theologians.

On the other side, for Cajetan, and for all Counter-Reformers, in addition to pure nature, the domain of philosophy and the human sciences, there existed a gratuitous supernature, the domain of dogmatic theology. This typical Renaissance *split* into two areas would ultimately prevail and become definitive, even among later Protestants. Human sciences and the "science of God" would now become separate disciplines. What had origi-

nally begun as a difference with regard to two diverse Christian
anthropologies would now become a rift between professional
theologians of the various confessions. The battle had shifted to
the theological heights, while in the lowlands of "pure nature"
anthropology won the field. Theology would progressively begin to employ a jargon which would be incomprehensible to lay
people from the human sciences. Anthropology, for its part,
could no longer tolerate any interference from the occult regions of "supernature."

Scientifically, the rupture between speech about God and
speech about human nature was thereby completed. Hencefor-
ward it was possible to reflect on the human condition without
relating it to God at the same time. And, on the other hand, people could theorize about God apart from human experience.
God and human beings became "substances" separate from
each other. The pagan concept of person had made its successful entrance into the whole of scientific thought including Aristotelian theology. The original Christian concept of relationship
was rejected. All of this explains the allergy of great Protestant
thinkers such as Karl Barth toward every form of "natural" or
purely philosophical doctrine of God which would be separate
from concrete biblical revelation. According to Barth, a Christian who reflects on the human condition must always see it
from the perspective of the ontological human connection with
God. And this is a relationship which we come to know only
through the revealing Word of God.

To say that God and human beings essentially or ontologi-
cally stand in relationship to each other in such a way that we
cannot adequately think about God apart from humans nor humans apart from God does not mean that this relationship
would be as immutable as a law of nature or a mathematical
function. This relationship is an initial given, and at the same
time a task to be realized historically.[7] As Karl Barth put it, it is
always "current," and is as unstable as a dialogue, a fight, or a

drama. "Every instance is an unexpected event: a victory or a defeat, resistance or fall, developing life or incipient death. . . . The relationship 'is' not there; it 'happens': on the part of God; in his choosing, his calling, his command, and his blessing; and on man's part, in his knowledge (faith) and his conduct (morality) which must continually be reformulated."[8]

Now Protestants (and all evangelical-minded Christians, really) have always been apprehensive about ascribing too much relationship-creating value to human activities or "works." For Protestants, as for Thomas before them, one's deeds are no more than the spontaneous consequence of one's manner of being: "Action follows being." The way leads not from doing to becoming or being, but in the opposite direction. One does not make oneself. Works or merits do not make one good, but a good person cannot help but overflow with good works. What is of fundamental value to a person becomes clear but does not depend upon that person's deeds. Whether or not I am a good person depends on what makes up the core of my person-ness, namely, my relationships. Others make me. I am shaped, not by the world or "the system," but by those with whom I know I am deeply connected in love, in dread, or in hate. Here a psychologist would speak of "the significant others." God gives me my being. People mold my character. I myself show the result through my works. I express outwardly what I have become interiorly through others.

Does this mean, then, that the human person would be the plaything of religious predestination or of psychological determination? For Luther, who, as Walgrave notes, "thinks more empirically-psychologically than philosophically," faith consists in the experience and acceptance of the fact that I am loved by God. Through acceptance of the relationship offered, I become "justified." The consequence of this "justification" is twofold. I experience that I am free of the law, and I realize that it is only now that I can love in freedom. Freedom from the law means being aware that my lot no longer depends on the correctness of my works, as I might have been inclined to think were I a Jew or a pagan thinking on a purely human level. "The experience of being justified and loved by God establishes ... not only freedom of a person, in reference to his works but also 'free works.' "9

The one who has been justified constructs his or her personality by entering into love relationships with others and with God, but this only comes about by virtue of knowing one is loved by God. In other words, love not only makes an unloved being into a loved being; it even makes one into a lovely being. In order to love in freedom, I must first have received love, gratis and unmerited, myself. A child who never received affection will not easily be able to give love. But anyone who has had the good fortune of experiencing love early starts to blossom like a plant in sunlight, even desiring to be able to give love in return. For this person, giving love is no longer a difficult task but a deep free desire. "Caritas" is a duty only for those who live outside the warmth of a living love relationship.

The difficulty for this view of things is that modern people very seldom feel that they have been addressed and struck by God's Word, and have scarcely any notion of being really loved by God. Many would very much like to believe this, but to experience it is an extreme rarity in our time. Most imagine that, as far as God is concerned, we are forsaken. They regard the human person as a solitary "substance." They are more likely to feel this "independence" as a liberation than as a lack. Through their eyes, it is a sober, realistic fact in every way. Their self-experience does not lie in the order of being but in the order of doing and having. The normal question is no longer: "Who are you, really?" Rather the modern question becomes: "What can you do? What do you own? What are you accomplishing?" This is the typically pagan experience of an altruistic person who has become self-centered. "He is aware of himself as a thing, and experiences himself in the body he has, in money, house, children, social position, in the power and problems that are his. . . . Instead of saying, 'I love my wife,' he says, 'I *have* a happy marriage.' "[10]

If a Catholic of the sixteenth century, according to Luther, suffered from "works righteousness," i.e., depended on personal merits, modern people measure an individual's worth almost exclusively from personal achievements. As long as people think individual worth can be measured by showing what one has, can do, and accomplishes, and not by who one *is* (i.e., with whom one is related and to whom one is called), we tend to feel that our society is "inhuman." It is seldom recognized that the real cause of all this is an anthropological misconception, a wrong view of the human person. What resentment does the average youth of our day express regarding contemporary life-style? Basically, youth protest today is directed against the same thing against which Luther four hundred and fifty years ago protested so vociferously, using, of course, more religious terminology: a person is not a merit-collecting achievement-oriented being, created only to work. A person is human not by an attitude of aggression or competition, but by an attitude of receptivity with regard to other people and the world, and, ultimately, with regard to God. "One of the guiding intuitions of contemporary thought," wrote E. Mounier, "is that existence is action, and superlative existence implies superlative action, definitely action."[11]

But the Christian sees action and achievement as a consequence of grace, not as cause for merit. It is because I experience and receive love that I can love. Because I received it, I can now also give it. It is because God came to me that I believe. But I do not come to faith *because* I first tried to be a good, honorable person. St. Bernard, long before Luther, had expressed this very thing when he said: "If it is possible for man to seek God and even to find him, then it is only because God always came first to him. For we could not even seek God at all, had he not already found us" (*De diligendo Deo*, VII, 22).

2. *Does Obedience Mean Alienation from Self?*

We often hear people say: "The Christian speaks glibly about person and freedom, but has the Church not often been the cause of a great deal of self-alienation?" Is not the basic cause of centuries of lack of freedom, of tutelage and alienation, to be found in religion itself? Generally speaking, we understand self-alienation as surrendering to someone else responsibility for what really belongs to the responsibility of my own conscience, and doing so out of a feeling of anxiety or incompetence, which is gladly labeled "obedience" or "modesty."

Those who regard religion as a source of self-alienation generally mean that personal decisions are exchanged for obedience to ecclesiastical authority or for principles of a "Christian morality." The alienated person then no longer acts from personal insight into good and evil, but from what others prescribe. Such a person "humbly" renounces the authority of individual conscience in order to take refuge under the safe umbrella of higher authority.

As a rule, these people forego all personal commitment in order meekly to await direction from above. They are no longer steering their own life's course; they are not even behind the wheel. Some are never even taught to drive. Others lost the ability long ago. Does not "public transportation" ultimately seem safer? Alienated people blindly follow their "master's voice." The "master" is no longer their conscience but a "foreign," external authority.

After Hegel launched the concept of self-alienation in a political context, Karl Marx took it over in his socio-economic writings. Since then, it has successively received a whole gamut of meanings, going from the worker who gets "alienated" from the products of his or her own work to the manager who is so *caught up* in managerial responsibilities that he or she gets alienated from every form of family and intimate life. Modern sociologists divide big-city life into public and private spheres. Depending on the degree to which a person rejects one of these two domains, out of either aversion or anxiety, we can speak of external or internal alienation, of one-sided introversion or of blatant extroversion. But here we only intend to examine self-alienation in terms of its being a direct consequence of religious systems, as it is sometimes regarded.

Religion, it is true, has sometimes promoted "external self-alienation." Some "schöne Seelen," beautiful souls as Hegel labels them, felt that they were encouraged again and again through pious meditation to leave the whole world of action, of science, of political and social life to others. Specifically, they were to be left to secularists so that they themselves might flee for safety to the domain of quiet interiority. Apparently, it completely escapes this sort of "stranger to the world" that extrovert commitment is an integral component of the human person. For these "pious" people, religion is apparently no more than the sterile interior decoration of their soul or anxious care for the enclosed garden of their "spiritual life." It is also against this kind of religion, a kind which alienates a person from action, that today's political theology, or theology of liberation, is turning. As long as societies operate in a dehumanizing way (and can one doubt it these days?) the person called to freedom must act in opposition to them and be committed to a better world. It is true that some prophets of the revolution forgot that no one can build a better external structure from an internal void. It is not social unrest but personal inspiration which builds up a positive, new order. Someone who no longer feels the ground under his or her feet is scarcely suited to offer others a better foundation.

It is remarkable, however, that, on the level of internal
alienation, the Christian religion has often caused the greatest
damage. Genuine Christianity does not operate in an alienating
way; quite the contrary, its intention is the liberation of humankind. But the existing religious institutions as they have developed historically, often growing out of shape, have repeatedly
taken away the most precious things an individual had: on the
moral level, the conscience, taken away in the name of "obedience"; and on the psychic level, the wealth of personal experience, denied in the name of exterior practices and obligations.

Let us consider the consequences of alienation of personal
conscience. Instead of judging and acting on the basis of personal experience, feeling, or insight, many resign themselves
submissively to the will of a "stranger." When they no longer
think for themselves, limiting themselves to faithfully carrying
out prescribed movements, they are then degraded to the position of a puppet or an actor who takes great care not to undertake anything personally. Their role is to play out as faultlessly
as possible a scenario prescribed by a "director." For such persons, the world is a theater. Each one of us plays a role and gets
a part.

In the past, many of the faithful resembled submissive actors more than creative personalities. Their lives were directed
by concrete ecclesiastical superiors or by abstract moral principles. The core of their humanity, namely, their conscience, un-
derwent a surgical operation or a spiritual "transplantation."
Someone else's—a stranger's—convictions and will were plant-
ed in them. Divorced from their personal conscience, they lis-
tened only to signals from someone else's will. The result was a
spiritual abdication which was misunderstood and camouflaged
as "obedience." Dostoevsky had his "Grand Inquisitor," his image of the authoritarian Church, explain why he required perfect
obedience; understandably, it was for the good of the people.
He took freedom of conscience from the people and based ev-

erything on authority. "Men rejoiced that they were again led like sheep and that the terrible gift that had brought them such suffering was, at last, lifted from their hearts. . . . The most painful secrets of their conscience, all, all they will bring to us, and *we* shall have an answer for all. And they will be glad to believe our answer, for it will save them from the great anxiety and terrible agony they endure at present in making a free decision for themselves."[12]

True Christian obedience, however, lies on an entirely different plane. In addition to the process of negative alienation by which I allow the core of my being a person (my conscience, my world of experience, my freedom) to be colonized by a foreign overlord whom I fear, there also exists a positive "alienation." I can allow "another" to be established in my heart, not from force or fear, but from love. This is not interference from a stranger or an alien, but rather an enrichment by another who releases me from being closed in on myself. In fact, I plant the one I love in my heart. The desires of the other no longer leave me indifferent or neutral. Love compels me to do or not do things regarding which I otherwise imagine myself to be "free." Love creates "bonds." The partner is no longer a stranger but takes possession of my person and becomes a part of myself. This does not enchain my freedom, but inspires and fructifies it.

From a distance, it may resemble a loss of autonomy, but one who has once tasted love knows no greater happiness than to give ear to the desires of the beloved. There is no greater joy than to be able to render a loved one happy. Only through the bond with the other do I really become myself. I do not find my "true identity" by breaking all bonds, but rather discover it through the influence of the "other," of someone whose unspoken wishes lay a hand on the formerly cold helm of my heart. Before, I did not know in which direction to travel. Now I have a "goal" and thus a task.

This is true not only on a psychological level between persons but also on the religious level with respect to God. In Christian perspective, I become fully human only after my consequence-laden encounter with God. It is this conviction which caused Luther to say: "Man is justified by faith." A person is saved only through faith in God. Or, in the words of a modern Protestant: "(Man) is reborn by the word of love. Faith therefore is not a virtue, which can be learned, but more like a process of birth. God's trust *engenders* trusting faith in men." Someone who has never felt personal change, never experienced the self becoming more fully its true self through the loving gaze of a friend, will not easily understand the experience of someone like Luther who knew he was loved and accepted by God. The interference of the "Other," who is God, not only does not limit my freedom; rather, it is what makes my freedom possible. "The experience of being justified and loved by God establishes . . . the freedom of a person."[13]

The experience of God's intervention in my life renders me more obedient (ob-audiens), more finely attuned to listen for something, or, better, for *Someone,* who escapes the unbeliever's notice. This listening takes hold of me to such a degree that it can no longer leave me unmoved; it changes me in all my doings. The Other takes possession of my heart. The Other enables me to answer "yes" in freedom. The mystic experiences all of this in a conscious way. The believer, on the other hand, knows this and believes it, though God's love is not so clearly or directly sensed.

Entering into the love of an Other is the only thing that makes a person free, even though one knows that the route begun means, at the same time, crossing over all other routes which were still possible before. In his novel *Steppenwolf,* H. Hesse describes how Harry, as an untameable wolf, "misunderstands freedom" as an "increasingly greater independence from everyone." It does not take long before the hero has to concede that a person bound to no one and therefore *with* no one goes aground on his solitary, "dis-obedient" independence. "But in the midst of the freedom he had achieved, Harry suddenly became aware that his freedom was a death and that he stood alone. The world in an uncanny fashion left him in peace. Other men concerned him no longer. He was not even concerned with himself. He began to suffocate slowly in the more and more rarefied atmosphere of remoteness and solitude. For now it was his wish no longer, not his aim, to be alone and independent, but rather his lot and his sentence."[14]

With Thomas Mann, we go yet a step farther in consequence of this view. This defender of an agnostic, ironical humanism makes it clear to what a cold form of solitude independence from other human beings, and from God can lead. When Cesare Pavese asserts that where classical art was religious, modern art is becoming more and more ironical, he means that, in his opinion, there are only two spiritual attitudes with which a person can maintain sufficient distance and reserve with respect to the material things around us: faith and irony. Neither of these two standpoints rejects the visible world, nor does either idolize it by entering totally into it. Both relativize concrete matter and therefore stand "above" it. One does it through its mockery and haughty disdain, the other through testing everything against the Absolute.

A. Hellensberg has summarized the tragedy of Mann's ironical distance and religious emptiness (of which the Nobel prizewinner was quite conscious) as follows: "In the center of his gaze there stands man, the failure, homeless, *having no ties,* alienated from himself and the world. The decisive figures of his novels seek to flee this condition, but they *fall back upon themselves.* Graceless, unsupported, trapped in themselves, they cannot perform the creative act of surrender to a higher reality."[15] Thomas Mann himself has not concealed his vain search for contact with the Other, for a liberating love of a higher order. Near the end of his life, he admitted in a Chicago lecture: "If it is Christian to perceive life, one's own life, as a guilt, indebtedness, obligation, as the object of religious uneasiness, as something urgently demanding reparation, salvation, and justification, then those theologians are not so correct with their assertion that I am typical of the a-Christian writer."[16]

A person feels guilt with respect to a "Someone." We obtain forgiveness from a Person. Thomas Mann, the apparently self-assured, conceited, ironical humanist that he was, really knew quite clearly what he was missing. His growing feeling of solitude made him look toward a saving "Thou," not in order to trade his autonomy, but in order to escape from an alienating loneliness.

3. *External Church Structures and the Interior Testimony of God*

The two privileged places of encounter between God and humanity, or, more exactly, the two places where the believer can get on the right track of God's will and God's call, are the exterior Church and the subjective interiority of each one's soul. The Church is *one* of the channels by which God addresses the listening person. Although we can never simply identify the word of ecclesiastical authorities with God's will, nevertheless Christ's word leaves no doubt about this: "He who hears you, hears me, and he who rejects you rejects me" (Lk 10:16). "Whatever you bind on earth shall be bound in heaven, and whatever you loose on earth shall be loosed in heaven" (Mt 18:18).

Once they are married, a man and woman, it is true, have many possibilities for meeting each other: they can travel together, go out for an evening, take a walk in a park, etc. But the privileged place will be their own home. If they rule it out as a matter of principle, or entirely refuse it, all other possibilities then become problematical and artificial. Similarly for the Christian, God's Church is the "divine milieu" par excellence. If the

Christian, for whatever reasons, rules it out, then and only then can the well-known adage be applied: "Extra Ecclesiam nulla salus" (Outside the Church there is no salvation). Through the ecclesially interpreted Word of God, the sacramental ritual, and the external structures of the Church, God has *willed* to make himself discoverable. God's Word has taken on "flesh" in this physical structure. The Invisible has willed to live "among us." The Eternal has entered into contingent history. In addition to this, there is the possibility for immediate contact between God and human beings. God also lets himself be found *outside* Church structures, directly, in the intimacy of everyone's interiority, in places and at times that are not fixed. With the coming of Christ, religion became an interior, personal matter as well an external, institutional structure. Hence, it is more than a question of external form, even though both continue to be necessary. "The hour is coming, and now is, when the true worshipers will worship the Father *in spirit and truth.* For such the Father seeks to worship him" (Jn 4:23).

Within the Church, the temptation of glossing over the interior testimony of God for the benefit of safer, more objective external testimony has cropped up time after time. Again and again there is the attempt to "brick up" the "temple of our soul" within the colonnades of the central Church building. The great masters of the spiritual life have continually shown their opposition to this chronic loss of interiority and of the personal, direct encounter with God. Luther, Erasmus and the Counter-Reformer Ignatius are vivid examples of this.

Luther never called the Church superfluous. His protest only went against the "reification" within the Church of the late Middle Ages. Religious symbols, or actual signs of our interior, direct relationship with God—as, for example, the host—were as a rule degraded to objective "things" at that time. People ascribed almost magical powers to external objects such as reliquaries, holy water, or devotional images. What was instituted

as a way to God became the terminus of short-sighted veneration. To a great degree the Church was reduced to an external
authoritarian organization with objective dogmas, concrete
practices and juridical requirements.

Protesting against this, men such as Luther, Erasmus and
Ignatius argued for the importance of an interior life which itself
would listen to God's word in the soul and which had an eye for
the transparency of religious "things." Things given religious
form were, for them, not "things in themselves"; rather they
were *signs* that pointed to God. In their eyes, alienation of personal interiority and inordinate dependence of exterior forms
had caused a genuine crisis of faith life. As has continually happened in the history of Christianity and of every other religion,
the scale had tipped almost entirely toward external form-giving. Interior inspiration, both on the moral level of personal
conscience and on the religious level of personal relationship
with God, appeared to be frozen. In the late Middle Ages, as
Huizinga attests, there was a "craving to turn every sacred idea
into precise images, to give it a distinct and clearly outlined
form. . . . By this tendency to embodiment in visible forms all
holy concepts are constantly exposed to the danger of harden-
ing into mere externalism."[17]

It was certainly not the goal of either the Reformers or of
the Counter-Reformers to achieve a "religion of pure spirit"
(Renaudet) that would deny or undervalue the importance and
the necessity of giving form to matter. Rather, they pointed out
that an external form such as, for example, the eucharistic
"bread" was not a "distinct, clearly-outlined thing" in itself but
an actual sign pointing to a Person. The Lord's intention in this
sacrament had to do not with bread but with his invisible Person. The external bread is a sign of the interior relationship.

Likewise, explicitly formulated moral principles should be
guidelines for the interior conscience, but never safe substitutes
for it. Now a sign is a thing raised "to the second power," or, in

other words, a thing which, taken up into the meaning attributed to it by a human culture, becomes a bearer of meaning, because, through this sign, Someone wants to share himself. Thus a letter is much more than a material thing consisting of paper and ink-marks. A letter is a thing that, when raised to the second power, is changed to "someone's word directed to me." Someone speaks to me via this "thing." If I keep and revere my friend's letter, it is not on account of the lovely paper or the novel color of ink but because of the fact that my friend used this everyday means in order to share with me something of his or her self.

Because of this, Erasmus calls a sacrament a "res media," a thing raised to the second power." In the first power it is, for example, paper and ink. Raised to the second power, it becomes the favorable inclination and the heart of my friend. Similarly, in the first instance, the host remains unleavened bread. In the second instance, my Beloved touches me directly through this (in itself common, even everyday) food. The great Church Reformers always protested against all fetishistic reverence of external "things"—the relics, the "letter" of doctrine or the matter of the sacraments. Their warning protests will probably never become entirely superfluous, because by definition religion depends on external symbolic form-giving in order to be able to put into words and images that which in principle transcends all words and images. It is so tempting to cling fast to the external when we know that it is impossible for us either to grasp or to comprehend the internal.

The Protestant Reformers were not the first in the Church to sound the alarm against reification, formalism, and the disappearance of free interiority. Already within the eleventh century medieval Church which was far more childlike and extrovert than the early Church of the Greek and Latin Fathers, there was a growing desire for more personal spirituality. The Carthusian Bruno, as well as the Cistercian Bernard and his Benedictine friend William of St. Thierry, consciously redirected the accent of liturgical pomp and of community exercises toward more personal prayer focusing on a personal relationship of the soul with God. Pilgrimages, penances, bodily fasting and physical efforts of every sort gradually began to give place to a more internalized ascent of the human soul to God.

If early medieval believers showed a childlike need to express their religious life by visible deeds and to externalize it by great accomplishments, the new masters of the spiritual life come forward as prophets of interiority. The non-monastic, urban piety of the Beguine movement and the "devotio moderna" of Thomas a Kempis or of Erasmus were eventually taken up and furthered by Ignatius of Loyola. The latter presented his "Spiritual Exercises" as an alternative to "monastic observance." It was only in the sixteenth century that this whole gradually-developing, "protesting," revival which faced reactionary opposition on the part of the Church apparatus would tragically lead to a rupture.

In addition to and independent from the Church which needed reforming but which was now considered definitively irreformable, an anti-Church arose with Luther and Calvin. The enormous emphasis with which the Reformation considered itself obliged to defend personal interiority impelled the Catholic Counter-Reform to undertake the difficult task of reminding believers of the well-known reverse side of the coin. The Catholic Counter-Reform affirmed that we do not have to let go of or to despise the exterior in order to preserve interiority. With a wary eye out for the danger of a "religion of pure spirit," the Catholic branch of Christianity had to defend the fact that a believer could give a material form to an inner experience. It insisted that "spirit" could express itself in "letter" for the reason that the human is at once a being endowed with language and bodiliness.

This was a thankless task, for the "Spirit" within the Christian world had lain smothered for ages under the dust of a lot of sophisticated practices, structures and "dead letters." Yet it is still true that every "protesting" prophet needs forms in order to be able to humanly express and to experience his relationship with God. Few have seen this as plainly as did the liberal Lutheran, Paul Tillich: "The first and fundamental meaning of Catholicism for the Protestant Churches lies in the fact that Catholicism has maintained the sacramental thought of the Church, namely, the notion that the Church represents the presence of the Divine, which is given, even before an individual experiences the divine in personal experience and action."[18] No matter how important personal experience may be, Tillich contends, God *is* already present, independently of that, in the visible Church. Hence, it is not religious experience which gradually expands into Church reform. Rather, it is the Church founded by Christ which makes Christian experience of God possible.[19] It is certainly striking that a contemporary Protestant comes to accentuate this primacy of the sacramental Church with respect to personal, interior relationship with God. Meanwhile, desire for interiority and greater profundity keeps taking root in the hearts of Protestants and Catholics at least insofar as they are serious about Christian life. Without this personal spiritualization, all Church life remains a "tinkling cymbal."

From Erasmus, who had consciously rejected the Protestantism of the "new" Church, up to our own time, the greatest Catholics would maintain the same basic concern, namely, for the priority of the Invisible over the visible, of the Spirit over the letter and of the personal over the organizational. Erasmus pleaded for a "true religion" of the "human person." In what did this ideal of his insight consist? Principally in the *transparency* of all outward forms: sacraments, dogmas, laws, images, ceremonies, etc. They are signs in which humans have always tried to express their being taken hold of by God. These form-givings, the "caro" of the "incarnation," are signs pointing to the Divine, i.e., toward the Spirit itself.

Hence, the encounter with God (Spiritus) is more essential than its objective exteriorization (caro).[20] The latter, like every cultural good, is historical and thus of a temporal nature and variable. The spiritual development of humanity, Teilhard's process of hominization," continually requires new forms. The humanistic person deserves credit for having the courage to remain creative. Clinging fast to temporal forms, which one then labels "eternal" or "willed so by God" is exactly what Sartre would call the "experience of bad faith."

Already with Erasmus we find in nucleus form the whole Christian personalism which must constantly take up arms against new forms of rigid and magical objectivism. The relationship of humans with God is not a relationship with a spring, a safe home, or a hope-giving horizon. For a Christian the face of a living, loving, and encountering God constantly emerges from behind the sacraments, the contingent Church structures and the "last things."

What comes first and foremost is the "visage of the Other, and all recourse to the word is already placed at the interior of the original face-to-face of the language."[21] Before dogmatic theory and before sacramental rites, there already existed the relationship of face-to-face between human beings and God. It is, however, a relationship which is and necessarily remains creative of words and forms.

· 7 ·

The Christian: One Called by God

1. *The Christian Concept of "Vocation"*

It has become commonplace to say that the people of today are in search of a "true identity." Modern culture abounds with such questions as: "Who am I, really? What is the purpose of my existence? What is my task? What route must I take in order to lead a life worth the effort? How do I find a meaningful place for myself in the world?" This cultural environment is all the more striking given the fact that we are just coming out of a period in which these issues were not questions at all, but, on the contrary, seemed self-evident.

For centuries, faith has offered answers to questions of identity and the purpose of life which at the most came up at moments of ultra-reflexivity or just before an important life-choice. Everyone felt safely sheltered in a cosmos which was interpreted religiously. Even though a person might not understand everything, he or she knew that somewhere there was a credible, cogent answer. Hence, there were no questions which were deeply perturbing.

But in our day, the riddle "What are we living for?" is no

longer a purely rhetorical question or an apologetical preamble to a brilliant Weltanschauung. Psychiatrists and other secularized successors of the "spiritual guides" of yesteryear can testify that anxiety neuroses and suicidal thoughts are becoming less exceptional and that increasing uneasiness about everything is affecting many. The question of meaning expresses itself in aggressive forms of protest, in pessimistic conservatism, or in milder forms of quiet boredom or of spiritual emptiness.

Questioning the meaning of existence does not so much arise from theoretical difficulties as from existential uneasiness. It is only when married life has lost its self-evidence that people begin to theorize about the meaning of monogamous, indissoluble marriage. It is not true that the majority of believers in former days could explain the meaning of obligatory Sunday celebration, but in our time they no longer can. Rather, something that was formerly self-evident and about which there was no need to speak or to reflect is now a problem. Anyone who questions the meaning of an existing structure is thereby expressing a hunger for something *new* rather than for better theoretical legitimizing of the old. The question of meaning does not arise just because certain theories appear to be no longer tenable. Theories arise only when self-evidence disappears. They are *a posteriori* defense mechanisms. Heresy, for example, is not an attack on existing dogmas. Rather, a dogma is a defense against heresy which is beginning to crop up.

The question of meaning emerges when the general feeling about life has changed and is in the process of developing into an uneasiness, a malaise. Until recently, the self-evident and general feeling about life that most people had was religious in nature. A handful of catechism texts sufficed to provide some understanding of the place of humanity in the cosmos, the meaning of life, and the task of the individual. By way of contrast, people of today no longer feel imbedded in self-evident "truths" provided by faith. New religious theories, much subtler and more understandable than those former catechism formulas, are less successful in convincing us that what former generations "spontaneously felt" would always be valid.

Religion has never been so widely discussed, theorized, and published as in our time. Nevertheless, all of this seems only to aggravate the crisis-situation. The teaching of religion was never renewed and adapted so much as now, and yet catechesis never seemed so powerless to provide any self-evidence for religion. The only thing that is self-evident is that our human identity has become insecure and problematical. No believer can be surprised at this. If people today began to feel more comfortable, at ease and happy within a milieu of increasing unbelief and secularity, that would be empirical proof that the believer's view of life had been a limiting and damaging one in the past. The ever-increasing emancipation of the person since the Enlightenment has had exactly the opposite effect. As God has disappeared farther behind the horizon, feelings of uneasiness, rancor, and meaninglessness have proportionately increased. If a satisfactory reply to the question "Who are we really?" could be given outside the context of faith, then it would be proof that faith is at most an accidental decoration, not essentially affecting the core of our being. But in reality, modern day questioners are clearly off the track in their search for the meaning of life.

From a cultural-historical point of view, people have, for centuries, looked at and understood themselves in the mirror of religion. Looking at that mirror, they supposed that they were reading in God's eyes who they were and why they existed. They understood themselves as having been "called by God." As the religious mirror got hazier, they began, in this search for self-understanding, to look for another mirror. They found psychology. Now, in psychology we read that humans are beings with certain qualities, character traits, frustrations, and complexes, searching for liberation from certain hankerings and for the greatest self-realization possible. Formerly, religion and morality, through priests and educators, specified what was good for us and what norms we had to observe. Today a popularized Freudian psychology fills this role. It specifies what is "normal," desirable, or outmoded. Where formerly preachers fostered anxiety about damage to the soul, now another type of person fosters just as much anxiety about dangers that might menace the body and "psychological balance."

Psychologists teach us that it is in the eyes of others that we read who we really are. Thus, anyone who experiences no human fellowship thereby also loses his or her true identity. Anyone who has become alienated from other human beings begins to suffer, ipso facto, from self-estrangement. In Christian language, we used to say that those alienated from God are denying their deepest selves and the very purpose of their existence. They become wretched sinners.

In our day those who are extolled by others consider themselves to be successful. However, public disapproval or disdain causes people to feel unsuccessful. Human opinion decisively shapes the self-understanding of the modern pagan. But the Christian believes that a person is ultimately worth what he or she signifies in God's eyes. "Beyond the precariousness of his identity, man is he whom God addresses."[1] Berger, therefore, sees the task of the Church as being a "place of truth," a place where a person no longer has to be concerned about the psychological or social labels attached by others, but where one comes to know one's worth and identity "in reality," that is, how one is seen by God. What else does an expression such as "Blessed are the poor of spirit" mean but that someone who passes for a wretch in the eyes of the world can be a privileged person in the eyes of God?

God's view of us, as we read in the Gospel, appears to differ vastly from the value judgment of "public opinion." For an answer to the question "Who am I, really?" the Christian turns in prayer to God. As far as the purpose of life is concerned, the same Christian believes that success or failure is a question of carrying out, or not carrying out, God's call. Here, life is understood as a spiritual adventure. It consists of a series of intentional events the meaning of which is only gradually revealed to us. It is by way of these providential events and concrete situations that God "calls" a person. The free decisions and choices whereby the Christian responds are made in the light of a "meaning" which one must learn to discover ever more clearly in life. For one does not create this "meaning" but receives it as having been offered or handed over. Ultimately, this meaning appears to be nothing other than entrance into relationship with Someone who calls a person because he cares for that person. It is a question of a call which can be responded to or not, satisfactorily or unsatisfactorily.

Hence, "accidental" circumstances such as talents, temperament, and occurrences that have a lasting effect not only shape the personality but also inspire and invite a response from the person. They are the concrete form in which God defines each Christian's duties of life from day to day. God uses actual circumstances to call each of us to concrete tasks. But God's invitational voice does more than point out a direction; it is accompanied by an inner power of attraction that we call "grace." Through external circumstances, God makes clear to the inwardly listening, obedient person what it is to which he or she is being called. The inescapable givens of our human situation define the boundaries within which we can find the happiness for which God has created us. The believer knows that for each person happiness is ultimately to be found only along the path intended by God and in the place where God awaits. Nevertheless, the human inclination always seems to be to seek elsewhere for this happiness, in competition with others or in the framework of purely human, transitory values.

"A person is brought forth by a call," according to Mounier.[2] A person acquires or becomes aware of a personal identity when that person is addressed or appealed to by another. It is through its mother's speech that the babe-in-arms becomes a child and develops a specific character. It is through the word that God addresses to us that we discover meaning in our personal life. Our "accidental" situation invites us to a reaction that is worth the effort. Life is no longer empty or absurd. It takes on a meaning because it seems that Someone needs me, or, rather, *wills* to need me. Since everyone's life situation is unique, every call to give an answer is also unique. Though in the eyes of the unbeliever this life situation came about accidentally through a concurrence of meaningless factors, a believer knows that it was "foreseen." It is meaningful and invites one in a well-defined direction. Henceforth it becomes each person's task to discover the path for one's own life ever more clearly and to do so within a prayer relationship.

We are each called from what we are to that which we must become in God's eyes. Our lives are a mixture composed of nature which determines us and of supernatural inspiration. Born into a situation which extensively limits us, we are now drawn by Someone who awakens new possibilities in us. Hence, nothing about us is accidental. We exist because from all eternity God has willed and dreamed us. We are neither "predestined" to absolute freedom and improvisation, as some existentialists would argue, nor, on the other hand, are we totally determined by biological and socio-cultural circumstances. In the context of our limited nature everyone is called by God along a way that can be accepted or rejected, followed or abandoned.

The richness of the biblical concept of "vocation" was gradually lost during the Middle Ages. At the end of this period it meant only that a minority of "chosen" Christians received an ecclesiastical function or were allotted a monastic status. In speaking of these persons as distinct from the "laity," people would say that they had a "vocation." In this way, three things disappeared from view. In the first place, it is not the Church but God himself who "calls" a person. As long as it is humans who "call forth vocations" the result will continue to be an unstable human fabrication. The vast crowd of the shipwrecked drifting on the seas of ecclesiastical life after the storms of recent years speaks for itself in this respect. It was Yahweh who "called" the Old Testament prophets. And the apostles became disciples only after a personal encounter with the Lord. Neither the prophets nor the apostles viewed their call as the magnanimous result of their sense of social responsibility. In other words, it was not out of social concern for the poor shepherdless folk that they became disciples. Nor was it because they thought that they had certain talents, psychological qualities or some "natural abilities" in themselves. Speaking of the vocation of the apostles, the poet Auden wrote: "No psychological background can throw any light on a calling which is initiated by God directly."[3] The apostles, in their surprise, followed Christ simply because he had called them, and for this reason only. The core of their vocation was not the question of what they might do for the good of the people entrusted to them, but the conviction that he had called them to speak in his name.

Secondly, the Christian concept of "vocation" is not limited to one definitive decision, made in one's youth, to "leave the world." Vocation is a permanent act which continues to concern a person at every moment of life, occasionally more acutely as in times of important decisions, and which is not only renewed but also more clearly specified each day. The vague route on which a person started out, full of good will, gradually becomes a concrete path with well-defined demands and renunciations. "Vocation" embraces one's entire life story. It is the story of a person choosing to live a life which, to the very end, is built on dialogue with an inspiring God. For the one who is called constantly comes up against new choices. That person knows that responses to those choices should never happen arbitrarily ("I choose what I want") but must happen freely ("I choose, and I know why").

True, life is not a continuous chain of new choices à la Sartre. Every life knows peak moments, moments when a person, at a crossroads, must risk taking a new day. Hammarskjöld calls them "points of no return." To see our life as a vocation, he said, is to understand that, in principle, we could go in many directions, but that happiness is to be found only along *one* path, specifically the path along which God calls us to go. "Body and soul contain a thousand possibilities out of which you can build many I's. But in only one of them is there a congruence of the elector and the elected. Only one—which you will never find until you have excluded all those superficial and fleeting possibilities of being and doing with which you toy, out of curiosity or wonder or greed, and which hinder you from casting anchor in the experience of the mystery of life, and the consciousness of the talent entrusted to you which is your *I*."[4]

Following your vocation, then, is a matter of continual choosing and consequently of following the way we began. Once the way is found, everything becomes simpler, at least as long as we do not retrace our steps. "There is a point at which everything becomes simple and there is no longer any question of choice, because all you have staked will be lost if you look back—life's point of no return."[5]

Just before his death Hammarskjöld fully realized that his life was not a self-construct or improvisation. "Life" had invited him, and he consciously entered into it. In fact, that became his happiness. On Pentecost 1961, in the last entry of his journal, he noted: "I don't know who—or what—put the question, I don't know when it was put. I don't even remember answering. But at some moment I did answer *Yes* to Someone—or Something— and from that hour I was certain that existence is meaningful and that, therefore, my life, in self-surrender, had a goal. From that moment I have known what it means 'not to look back' and 'to take no thought for the morrow.' Led by the Ariadne's thread of my answer through the labyrinth of life, I came to a time and a place where I realized that the Way leads to a triumph which is a catastrophe, and to a catastrophe which is a triumph. . . . Asked if I have courage to go on to the end, I answer Yes without a second thought."[6]

The third thing that was lost in the medieval concept of vocation, an oversight that has been an important part of later Catholic tradition up to our own days, was the fact that laity, too, are "called" in a personal way. It was Luther and Calvin who would rescue the biblical idea of vocation from the narrow, private possession of monks and priests. "Luther insisted that every lawful occupation was a vocation in the sight of God and that the individual ought to apply it to the same earnestness that was expected of a priest, a monk, or a nun in the performance of their calling. The Calvinist Reformation further intensified this understanding."[7]

Not only religious or ecclesiastical, but profane work, too, was regarded by the Protestants as a vocation. As M. Weber in his book *Protestantishce Ethik und der Geist der Kapitalismus* has shown, the important result of this was that from the sixteenth century on, Western civilization would develop a totally new attitude toward work. Seriousness about one's calling now took on a religious, almost Puritan, undertone. For example, early rising and hard work assumed moral and even religious significance. It became something holy to succeed in one's work. Capitalism, too, could record its greatest economic success in Puritan Protestant northern Europe and North America, in those very lands where the immediate pleasures of life had to give way most clearly to a strong work ethic on account of religious motives. It is, incidentally, the same lands that in our days draw the strongest reactions on the part of hippies and beatniks. What revolutionary youth abhor more than anything is moral puritanism, strict fulfillment of obligation, economic progress, and capitalism.

After the Reformation, and more specifically since the Enlightenment, this understanding of a vocation "in the world" gradually began to lose its religious depth once more. People approached their "work" or their vocational task less and less as a "Christian vocation." A vocation was then regarded not so much as a "call" as a "job" or "breadwinning." Being a believer became more and more a private matter separated from the function or the office one held in profane society.

Faith, as it were, became a private option for one's free time. Vocational life, on the other hand, was viewed soberly and realistically as a business affair. One maintains a distance from one's work, even becoming "alienated" from it (Marx). Fewer and fewer identify themselves with their employment. The consequence of this is that a person has less of a sense of the purpose of existence. And so the modern man or woman goes in search of his or her "true identity," asking the question, "Why are we living?"

This modern tendency to secularize goes so far, in fact, that people even begin to regard ecclesiastical tasks such as the priesthood as a function rather than as a vocation. It becomes a function which, under certain circumstances, one can "lay down," for example, when its social utility no longer seems evident, or when someone's "psychological balance" would suffer under it. Since secularization, a person's life task becomes a question of temperament, preference, and accidental circumstances. One chooses a way of life which promises the greatest psychological comfort and the most secure social future. But a genuine believer does not appropriate a task or mission to oneself. God chooses and calls in sovereign freedom and with striking diversity. It is because of this that people, and thus their vocations, are fundamentally different and unique. But each of us is free to respond. We can also go our "own way."

Is the one who "listens" to God's call, then, the unimaginative character in a predestined scenario? Would God have traced out a course that one must scrupulously follow through the jungle of life? Paul's answer is clear: "You were called to *freedom*. . . . For freedom Christ has set us free" (Gal 5:13. 1). The only "law" with respect to vocation is the call to love. This love, which God wants to awaken to full bloom in us, includes two things. First, love is a question of "election," that is, of a "preference" for Someone. This preference marks each of us. What I ultimately prefer constitutes the value of my life, or its failure since a person can prefer banal values and give up everything for them. "The first and most precious thing in man is his preference. It is *that* which God wants to have, so that he would be chosen with love above all that he has created or may create."[8] In fact, God wants to be loved "above all things."

Secondly, love is always creative and inventive and in that lies its freedom. The Beloved does not prescribe for me what I have to do. That, on the contrary, is what a tyrant would do. The Beloved only asks that I attune what I do to him, that I be mindful of him, and, especially, that I be where he awaits me. "Free works . . . are works freed from the purpose and the necessity to justify oneself." They occur "spontaneously, unselfishly, as if playing. . . . That so-called new obedience is new only when it is no longer obedience but free, imaginative, and loving." We are called to "the play of love which does the right whenever it does as it will."[9] To follow one's vocation, then, becomes a question of creative love, a love that does the most beautiful thing one can do with the talents, circumstances and inspiration, which are not given by accident, of life. One's gaze remains fixed upon the best-Beloved.

2. *The Search in Freedom for One's True Vocation*

In which direction must one move in order to reach one's

destination? How do we find out what God expects of us? Where does a person learn to know God's will? God's inspiration is learned only in moments of introversion. Prayer alone makes it possible to distinguish between the spontaneous desires of human nature and God's inviting voice. One who understands one's life as a vocation can take advice or turn to more sober criteria such as temperament, the needs existing in the world, psychological self-knowledge, and personal preference. These are not "accidental" signs and can be significant.

But ultimately a mature decision is made only in dialogue between God and the person who has turned within, who has been introverted. Since the Spirit of God sometimes "touches" the person who prays in a direct manner, this person must be attentive to the "movements" caused by the Spirit on the surface of the soul. Here Ruusbroec speaks of a "hidden whispering in our inward ear." "By it we become suited to hear the truths which the Spirit of God wants to make known to us interiorly, and to take them up into ourselves. . . . In this way (the Spirit) makes it clear to us how we should feel interiorly and how we should conduct ourselves outwardly, if we want to follow Christ."[10]

The final rule of conduct for a person's vocation is this "hidden whispering of God" and "God's touch" in the human soul. But the sober psychologist knows that the human psyche can be "touched" by the most diverse, the most banal and profane, "movements" or influences. This is why Ruusbroec insisted so emphatically on the necessity of "one's own discretion," that is, one's personal discretion or faculty to discern between right and wrong, between reality and psychological appearances, between the inspiration from God and the product of my fantasy. It is here that Ignatius speaks of *discrecion de espiritus* or discernment of spirits. In a number of "rules," he teaches the person of prayer to distinguish between "movements" in the human psyche which are characteristic of the work of God's inspiration, and "movements" which are certainly not to be trusted. A reading of Ignatius' autobiography and of his spiritual journal clearly shows that the man, in his prayer, always let himself be led by his *experiencia de la diversitad de espiritus* (experience of the diversity of spirits). Important decisions (*elecciones*) were taken only when he received the certainty that God and not "another spirit" was moving and driving his soul. He was definitively cured of a temporary scrupulosity only after he saw "with great clarity" that the thoughts and feelings which then came over him showed not a single characteristic that would be typical of God's work in the soul. Then he resolutely rejected any further conscious consideration of them. Ignatius' "rules for discernment of spirits" have been correctly called "a critical discipline of that sensibility which is the necessary and very rich point of departure of all psychological life, and, hence, of spiritual life."[11]

Does Ignatius then base the spiritual life on sentiment and emotions? Quite the contrary! Instead of taking feelings such as contentment, spontaneous dislike, and sadness as criteria for what is good or bad for a person ("For years now I have been feeling discontented in the priestly life, so I have not been made to be a priest"), Ignatius *relativizes* all psychological states. It is only indirectly that he ascribes a value to emotional ups and downs. They can be *signs* of something deeper. Therefore, they require correct interpretation. It is not psychology which is our rule of conduct. Our rule of conduct is God.

Well, God, and the evil spirit as well, touches us in the noblest gift we received from the Creator: our psyche. Joy or sadness, peace or anxiety, far from being the only things that matter, can be *signs* by which God calls his beloved writer to himself. The thing to do is to find out their meaning. "The discernment of spirits," then, means to believe that there is more in the human person than emotional life and thoughts. According to Ruusbroec, the task of "discretion" is to find out whether

what I feel and think is really in accord with the deepest level of
my being. For it is in the center of the soul that God touches,
addresses, and, above all, "calls" each of us. Not all spiritual
emotions, religious notions, desires, and pious plans are a faithful reflection of God's will. That is why a believer will carefully
test emotional and rational "movements" in order to distinguish
God's inspiration properly. The beleaguered Job did not escape
adversity; his sorrow did not cause him to change his course.
Quite the contrary. Behind the clouds of his trials, which certainly were not accidental, he tried to make out God's intention.
The "night of the senses" was similarly not an occasion for John
of the Cross to leave his grim path as soon as possible. He
learned to interpret the dark solitude in which he found himself
as a "sign" that God was calling him more intimately to himself.

Ignatius of Loyola understands "movements of the soul" to
include emotional states as well as thoughts, subtle reasonings,
desires, images that present themselves, savor, aversion, etc.
Great lucidity is necessary in order to prove and to test these
states of consciousness. Here the great enemy is illusion. In other words, there is the danger of falsely ascribing to God that
which really has its origin in egocentric needs or psychological
projections, namely, in the sphere of influence of the "bad spirit." "The spiritual person . . . ought with great watchfulness and
care to examine and to distinguish (everything). . . . It is necessary that all its various resolves and plans . . . be thoroughly well
examined before they receive entire credit and are carried out
into effect. . . . We ought to be very careful to watch the course
of (our) thoughts."[12]

A person who lives spiritually gradually acquires more experience in this, eventually achieving almost intuitive certitude.
When Ignatius sums up the psychological characteristics of
God's work within each person, he first of all bases his state-
ments on his personal experiences of anxiety and joy at Man-
resa. He knows, however, that his insights are not new: they lie

imbedded within the secure dikes of the whole stream of Christian tradition, beginning with the New Testament. What Ignatius finds typical for geniune inspiration we discover again in so many words in the works of the fourteenth and fifteenth century Devotio Moderna, "Modern Devotion," such as, for example, in Gerlach Peters' *Soliloquium,* in Ruusbroec's phenomenology of the spiritual life, in Athanasius' biography of St. Anthony, and even in the epistles of Paul and John.

The contribution of Ignatius in this area lay not so much in his originality as in his daring. It certainly required courage for him in a time of autocratic clericalism to affirm that God often calls people unto himself by working directly in the individual soul and not only through representatives of the official Church. Ignatius neither discovered this in the Bible nor dug it out of tradition. In his conversion he had himself experienced it. Knowing how easily a person becomes a victim of pious delusion and scrupulous anxieties, he tried to be as precise and clear as possible in his phenomenological description of what is genuine and what is false.

What are the signs of God's direct operations in the soul? What goes on within a person's mind when he is moved or addressed by God? This person experiences joy, peace, *se-curitas* (absence of worry), *dilatatio cordis* (expansiveness of heart), courage, strength, and "inspiration." One enters a condition that makes everything seem easier and appears to remove all obstacles from the way. Putting it in one word, Ignatius called this spiritual state *consolatio* (consolation). The soul "burns with love" for its Creator. It experiences faith, hope, and love intensely. It feels spontaneously attracted by "heavenly things."

In contrast to this, the characteristics of illusion are confusion, restlessness, agitation, interior tension and especially *angustia cordis* (anxiety). If a person of prayer enters such a state, then Ignatius speaks of "diabolic influences" against which one must not try to fight; still less should one act upon them. In his

Life of St. Anthony, St. Athanasius speaks of a "troubled, agitated spirit, restlessness of soul, chaotic thoughts and dimness or dullness of emotions."

The New Testament, too, speaks of this diversity of spiritual influences: "Beloved, do not believe every spirit, but test the spirits to see whether they are of God" (1 Jn 4:1). The "discernment of spirits" is also close to the heart of St. Paul (cf. 1 Cor 12:10). "The fruit of the Spirit is love, joy, peace, patience, kindness, goodness, faithfulness, gentleness, self-control" (Gal 5:22). Whenever Christ appears in the Gospel, peace and joy are always promised and fear is banished: "Be not afraid! Why does anxiety arise in your heart? Why are you so afraid?" In his spiritual journal compiled at the beginning of the fifteenth century, Peters writes: "There is no more evident indication or clearer sign that one is united with Christ than that, free of all anxiety, one walks in interior spaciousness." "Fear" always comes about from "taking appearances for reality. Fear never arises in the spiritual life unless it be where Truth is absent." In other words, anyone getting anxiety-producing thoughts knows that this inspiration does not come from God, for God calls no one to himself through fear.

Ignatius goes on to firmly dissuade a person from making a decision with regard to vocation, or from introducing any change in the way of life that has been chosen, as long as one is still in "desolation." God's voice in calling a person always works to extend freedom, to render the person happy, and to grant further enlightenment. Periods of "desolation" or confusion are not necessarily signs of infidelity or of alienation from God, although under certain circumstances they could contain a warning. Ignatius distinguishes three reasons for which a person is at times left in spiritual desolation or even anxiety. In the first place, desolation can be the result of religious laxity or infidelity. In that case it serves as handwriting on the wall. Second, a believer who feels forsaken should ask whether his or her previous prayer was pure or not. Was that prayer just eager for devout emotions, or did it remain directed toward God even after "devotion" went away? Desolation then is a time of purification. Third, desolation points to the fact that genuine prayer can only be God's own work since, left to ourselves, we appear to be incapable of anything substantial. A person in desolation learns how true Paul's word is: "No one can say 'Jesus is Lord' except by the Holy Spirit" (1 Cor 12:3).

Now does this mean that Ignatius, and the whole Christian tradition upon which he draws, should be considered as propagators of a sort of psychological cheerfulness or spiritual optimism? Do they simply intend to keep us from losing courage in "this valley of tears" in spite of everything? Not at all. What they are *really* concerned about is the *relativizing* of happiness and sadness, joy and anxiety. What for superficial people is the only experience, namely their mood, becomes for a believer something relatively unimportant, for the latter is able to look at everything from a deeper standpoint.

Something happening on the surface of the soul's life can be a sign that there is something wrong on a deeper level. But this does not have to be the case. Therefore, the surface phenomena must be tested and examined. In stormy weather a submarine continues to be very sensitive to waves as long as it rides along the surface of the water. Once it is entirely submerged, it becomes insensible to the wildest tempests ravaging the surface of the sea. In calm serenity it travels on into deeper levels of the ocean. Not all ships reach or even know these depths. Similarly, not everyone knows how to relativize emotional states. In order to do that, something "absolute" is required. A certain "depth" is necessary to which everything else can be referred. Psychological states of consciousness are not meaningless but their meaning for a spiritual person is of an *in*direct sort. Such a person is not struck more forcefully by them but he will feel freer with regard to personal feelings in proportion as greater spiritual depths are reached.

The spiritual person, therefore, is a free person, a person characterized by what the medieval mystics called "liberty of spirit": the freedom of perfect love. Ruusbroec describes this as "a care-free freedom" and "a strong resistance to pleasure or pain." In other words pain and pleasure are no longer able to shock the believer, the core of whose being lies anchored in God's rest. The believer's love-experience with God is more deeply gripping than anything else in the world. All the rest is thereby relativized.

This, however, does not mean that a believer would pass through life unmoved or lacking interest. Nature, everyday things of life and even the promptings of personal emotions touch this believer through and through and are experienced without escaping to the safe shelter of a "spiritual depth" alien to the world. Like Bernard and Francis, countless other great Christians have been led to emotions of wonderful elevation and gratitude by the beauty of nature. In it they have seen the hand of the Creator.

Concerning the movements in one's emotional life, Ignatius noted that it is not *knowing many things that satisfies and fulfills the soul, but rather the interior feeling and sensing of things"* (*sentir y gustar las cosas internamente*). Though God is far more important than my experience of him, spiritual writers nevertheless attach great importance to the adequate description of the psychological experience itself. Less precious senses, such as touch and taste, are preferred to the more exact senses of sight or hearing. The former leave more room for the undefinable mystery of God's almost imperceptible presence. God never seizes us in an overbearing or obtrusive way. He often "touches" us, but only a "quiet" person becomes aware of it. Through nature and the motions of one's experiential life a believer recognizes God's discreet invitation, or rather discovers his or her personal vocation.

It is striking how soon after his death the Counter-Reformation began to silence this core of Ignatian spirituality and to hide it away under the tombstone of ecclesiastical prudence. It was not long before people would venerate the "letter," objective and applicable to each and every one, more than the Spirit operating within the human subject. The official doctrinal authority, in fact, often branded "discernment of spirits" as dangerous and suspicious out of fear of illuminism, Protestant "free interpretation," or extra-ecclesial subjectivism. "The reason why there are so few really free Christians, adult Christians, virile Christians, so few real men, is because too often this immediate action of God, this essential and primordial role of the Holy Spirit, the interior Master, is badly known, forgotten, and—for certain people, pharisees, we could even say—feared."[13]

Ignatius' third successor as Superior General of the Jesuits, the Belgian Mercurianus, in an official letter was already discouraging his subjects from any mention of "discernment of spirits." To be specific, he regarded it as much wiser to make decisions regarding vocation only on grounds of "rational insight" and "intellectual consideration." And in the nineteenth century, the famous Jesuit Superior General Aquaviva would insist that finding out God's call is "safer and more prudent through discursive reasoning and reflection."[14] Between the years 1607 and 1882, the year Gagliardi rediscovered Ignatius' method of "discernment," the very core of Ignatian spirituality continued to be left out of all reprintings of the *Spiritual Exercises*. The high tide of rationalism and the Counter-Reformation's fear of any "free interpretation" of God's word had brought the Church to begin to distrust the "interior testimony" of the Spirit of God. The result of this is that vocation became an impersonal and objective matter.

But the relationship between two persons is not a physical

object; it is not a "thing" capable of being grasped by pure intellect. Centuries of "religious rationalism," if this concept is not
an all too crass contradiction in terms, have brought part of today's Christendom to rediscover the "pneumatic" or "pentecostal" aspect of religion with considerable passion. In a number of
"charismatic movements," the stream of religious life suddenly
overflows the banks of ordered rationalism. Whether at the
same time the "spirits" are always critically tested is a matter
outside of our scope here. What is certain is that we cannot try
to hold the Spirit of God on a leash of impersonal thinking. The
Spirit of God blows where he wills, which incidentally is not to
say that *every* breeze is a sign of God's speaking.

If we hold it possible that there can be direct and personal
contact between God and individual persons, that can open the
door to quite a number of pious illusions, aberrations, and pseu-
do-illuminations. This is why it is so important that the distinction between illuminism and actual experience of God be
outlined precisely. The cult of one's own ego is typical of illuminism. That ego wants to be the recording center for all sorts of
extraordinary and "interesting" experiences. Here, it is my experience and not God which counts as the most precious treasure. An *illuminato,* of the twentieth as well as of the sixteenth
century, is always in search of new waters upon which he or she
can drift in a way that is less tied down, more expansive, and,
especially, more spiritually brilliant. "Discernment of spirits,"
however, only becomes possible when the "I" has given up all
egocentric search for the enrichment of its own psychological
life. The central point here is the will of the Other who calls me.
The *illuminato* and the "discerning" person both devote much
attention to what is going on in their own soul and hence give
less consideration to principles, objective laws, and sober advice
from authority. But the "discerning" believer seeks to "discern"
what God wants. This believer knows that God lets himself be
encountered in the soul and can be "heard" there rather than,

for example, in astrology or in palm-reading. For this person, the life of the soul is not an end in itself; it is a stage on the way to God. But the "illuminated" person cultivates the life of the psyche for its own sake, even while gladly using jargon which sounds religious at the same time.

No matter how ambiguous the concept "discernment of spirits" may sound to some ears, we are justified in retaining this biblical terminology for historical reasons. One difficulty, of course, is that it often makes one think of Manichaean splitting of reality into two spheres of influence, spheres controlled by good and evil spirits respectively which compete with each other for the human soul. The *discretio spirituum,* however, is first of all a form of personal prayer, a "dialogue" between God and the soul. Speaking more phenomenologically, it is an intuitive power of judgment following on a free choice of the human will with regard to one's vocational path in life. It is also the subsequent determination, made in faith, whether a person has chosen well or badly, i.e., whether it was God's inspiration that was followed and not personal whims.

Chronologically, the prayer of one trying to discern God's will runs through several stages. In the first stage, a person of prayer seeks God's will in an unbiased manner (i.e., detached from personal preference, free of prejudices). Here Ignatius speaks of "indifference." One "tests" various possibilities. By using the imagination to venture along a proposed path, the individual measures the effects of each possibility. Does the thought of one course of action make this person more calm than anxious? With this question our inquirer is already in the second stage. Each of the various possible options had a different effect on the disposition of the soul. Therefore, this person pays close attention to the "movements" experienced in prayer. These "movements" were not cultivated, nor were they evoked or maintained by personal efforts. They are examined as to their psychological origins or possible "Cause." It is only in the latter case, when the source is experienced as a "Cause" beyond the self, that one can *know* that one is on the threshold of the right path. Therefore, the person now ultimately *chooses* that path, voluntarily choosing the way that has already brought peace and joy in the process of prayerful consideration.

After the will's choice made in faith or abandonment of the will to God, there now follows a third stage. A person now experiences and knows, with intuitive certitude, that the choice was the right one, even though the "why" cannot always be formulated in an understandable way. As Peter said: "Now I am *sure* that the Lord has sent . . ." (Acts 12:11). Or in Ionesco's words: "I was seized by an overflowing joy and I said to myself: Now, whatever happens, I *know*. I will always remember that moment."[15]

Turning one's back on a life option once taken in faith is what the believer experiences in apostasy. Here Ionesco speaks in terms of a "fall." The cause of this "fall," whether from faith, from a vocational choice, or from the word given to the One who "called," is always the same: one no longer *feels* what one felt back in the moment of choice. One no longer feels the same certainty, calm, and enthusiasm. Perhaps at that time, one may have chosen those pleasant feelings rather than God, who had made his way clear through those feelings. For each person there are moments in which fidelity, both to God as well as to any others with whom one was called, is no longer experienced in the spontaneity of the original enthusiasm. "The 'Yes' is a burden; it is agreed to without love."[16]

The person of prayer, however, may not call into question the existence of the sun when only clouds can be seen. The "discernment of spirits" thoroughly relativizes the feelings accompanying it. There are states of the soul in which God calls a person to something new. His call is concretized. In joy and peace the believer is called yet "further." The relationship with God becomes closer and more intimate. Periods of aridity and darkness also occur, periods in which God asks only for fidelity and perseverance. New decisions or changes of course are out of the question at such times. The believer assents to God's call only in the light of God's sensible presence evidenced by feelings of peace and calm. That assent, however, should not be suspended or placed in doubt at a later time when one is in a state of anxiety. It is usually during periods of desolation that a person is tempted to be unfaithful to a chosen vocation. At such times the person no longer sees any light in the choice that has been made—as if a responsible choice for God could occur without his light!

Through the "discernment of spirits," then, the person of prayer seeks and discovers ever more clearly God's will for his or her life. At the same time, the ability to experience the Lord's inward operations and to learn discernment remains pure grace. It has to do with an experience of consolation which comes over a person passively, "without any preceding cause."[17] It is a form of prayer which cannot be acquired or learned by any ascetical practices. It is not a devout method or "a psychological technique" that can be "tried out" by someone in doubt in order to receive clarity in decisions that have to be made. For the "discernment" of the Spirit of God presupposes two conditions: an interior life of prayer and a decision taken once and for all solely to seek some clarity about one's path of life in dialogue with God. What the individual wants is no longer the decisive consideration, but what the Lord wills.

To the degree that this is true, the believer may confidently expect that God will in fact make his will clear. It is by reading the state of our own soul that we can know whether we are living in God or from egocentric motives. In the latter case, anxiety creeps over us. Naturally, "if the soul cannot always breathe in this freedom and broad spaciousness, but for some reason it is weighted down and anxious, then this never comes from God: the 'self' has once again cropped up, drawing a narrow cell round about itself, and cutting a person off from that *latitudo* (spaciousness)."[18] One can tell "in his psychological center" whether one is being inspired by God or by worldly motives instead. The rule of thumb in this matter is no longer the word of Church authority or the text of a spiritual treatise. The guiding principle is God's direction operation within the soul, an "intervention" which has to be constantly and carefully recognized and interpreted by the person of prayer.

Our present time is especially sensitive to the communitarian aspect of religious life. The question, therefore, comes up, and is answered positively by man, as to whether there can be any such thing as "communal discernment of spirits." In other words, can a *group,* also, be moved and prompted, as a group, to take certain options? And, since it would be difficult to deny this possibility, can one say more specifically that discernment of spirits can be experienced on a *community* level without being unfaithful to its very core which is the direct, *personal* relationship between the individual human being and God?

The "Centrum Ignatianum" in Rome has collected all literature giving a positive reply to this question in a "Dossier Deliberación."[19] The dossier does not consider whether it is possible in principle to insert discernment of spirits into a more communitarian form of prayer, thereby extending it to the social level in which people of our day are particularly interested. Perhaps it would be worth a try. It is quite certain, however, that this was never the intention of Ignatius. For him as for the other great masters of the Christian prayer life, the fact that the individual believer can be addressed directly and personally by God was unquestionably a value worth defending. The Lord speaks not only through the hierarchically structured group or Church. He also addresses himself directly to the soul praying in stillness. Because the objective Church can guarantee nothing in this realm, the believer must test for himself or for herself and discern whether he or she is actually dealing with God and not with psychological illusions, passing moods, or "evil spirits." And here "discernment of spirits" is the only guide.

The fact that the post-war sensitivity for personalistic philosophies is presently being supplemented by and at times even exchanged for doctrines which sound more social does not diminish the central importance of this *personal* encounter with God. It is of course evident that the person is also a social being, and, as such, is also member of a community, namely, the Church. But it is typical of Christianity that the community may never (no matter how often this, alas, may have happened historically!) sacrifice one of its members for the social well-being of the group. No personal vocation may be hindered or stopped in the name of the welfare of the Church. On the contrary the traditional *personalistic* form of the discernment of spirits has great importance for the social and communal life of the Church. Even though it has always been this way and it is by no means a new discovery arising from our modern sensitivity, a contemporary example may clarify this.

More and more believers seem to be in a state of panic regarding the future of the Church and even of the Christian faith. They are concerned and upset when they see how many are leaving the Church and how few feel called to a specifically ecclesiastical "function." They are speechless at the number of those living with doubt and uncertainty about faith values formerly considered impregnable. People wonder how, humanly speaking, we can look forward to any rose-colored future for the Church. In fact, anyone examining what is happening in the Church from a purely sociological and psychological point of view cannot escape the impression that the Church demonstrates many characteristics of a business taking a turn for the worse. It appears to hold very little attraction for persons who might possibly be sympathetic toward it.

The normal consequence of this purely human view of the Church as a social phenomenon is concern, anxiety, and discouragement. These are the very emotions which, as Gerlach Peters, Ignatius and many others would say, render a correct faith outlook on events *impossible.* It is well known that, for the evangelist, "the little boat in the storm at sea" was a symbol of the Church in need. When the little boat threatened to capsize, the apostles were seized with great fear. "Form history" tells us that they were afraid of persecution of the Church, a persecution which threatened everything in the first century after Christ. What would be left of the Church? That was the anxious question of the young, primitive Church.

Today the Church seems to be "persecuted" more by growing indifference than by political repression or physical power. But the spontaneous reaction is the same as before: anxiety, doubt, and hopelessness. Such emotions, current especially in ecclesiastical circles, must also be "tested" and "discerned." Just as in matters of individual concern, worry and confusion in community concerns can certainly be bad counselors. Christ's word "Why are you afraid? Have you no faith" (Mk 4:40) is still applicable in the twentieth century. Christ regarded fear of the future of the church and hesitation about the durability of Christianity as synonymous for "not yet possessing genuine faith." It is therefore synonymous for taking a purely human view of the matter, whereas an "aspectus interior," an inner outlook, to use Gerlach Peters' expression, is necessary if we want to understand what is going on "in truth."

That is why the testimony of someone such as Roger Schutz is so much more worthy of belief than that of many ecclesiastical "messengers of Job." Schutz's speaking and writing betray neither fear nor anxiety, but instead a great lucidity. He judges everything with the gaze of one who knows that "there is no such thing as fear except where the truth is not seen" (Gerlach Peters). Dostoevsky says the same thing: "Anxiety is actually nothing but the consequence of lies."

Seeking the truth constitutes the very core of the "discernment of spirits." Thus, human emotions such as fear arising in a faithful believer—in, for example, a discouraged priest or an aging monk or nun distressed by what is happening or is no longer happening in the Church—must be "discerned in prayer." Only then will the Christian again be able to live as (according to Paul) he *must* live: "in joy." This is certainly not an infantile joy which does not dare look the situation in the eye, but a believing joy which sees *more* than sociological, statistical or psychological trends. Today as well as yesterday, Christ's words, "Why are you troubled, and why do questionings arise in your heart?" (Lk 24:38), are an exhortation not to trust *every* emotion that might arise in a believing heart. "Discernment" well becomes a believer.

3. *Differences of Vocations*

No matter how shocking it might sound to the ears of a modern democrat, for whom "all men and women are equal," vocations viewed in Christian perspective are basically unequal. Not only is everyone's life-path different from every other, but these paths were also foreordained to be unique.

Now, vocations can differ in a twofold way. In the first place, there are objectively different juridical states of life such as marriage, celibacy, contemplative monastic life, educator, lay brother, and so on. Subjectively, too, the degree of intimacy with God to which one is called can differ, for not all devout persons are mystically graced.

As we mentioned before, it was rediscovered by the Reformation that every juridical state of life must be interpreted as a Christian vocation. In other words, it is incorrect to maintain that some privileged souls would be "elected" for an ecclesiastical function whereas all others would have to move along their life course on their own hook. This would mean that ecclesiastical functions would be a matter of God's will, and profane vocations or states in life would be a question of temperament and talent.

Insight into God's will and psychological and social considerations are relevant to *all* states of life. The Christian's vocation is neither a purely supernatural matter nor a simple question of personal interest and chances of success. *Every* state of life can be chosen from a deeper inspiration just as *every* function can be chosen out of purely human calculation. Realizing that personal temperament, life-circumstances, and talents are not accidental "signs" through which God makes his will known, the Christian soberly seeks to move *from this context* to the place to which God's call is leading.

From time to time we hear it asserted that voluntary celibacy is the result of an unnatural (if not *anti*-natural) effort of the will. In reality, neither fidelity in Christian marriage nor perseverance in celibacy is a "natural" phenomenon. Both require supernatural inspiration if they are not to degenerate into caricatures. Both forms of life presuppose passions and desires that are, in fact, more than natural. In both instances a person will have to go counter to quite a few natural impulses in order to be faithful. In both cases, the *only* natural "given" in both instances is that almost everyone persistently desires an attractive member of the opposite sex. It requires supernatural inspiration and strength to go from this positive animal impulse to the construction of a Christian marriage or to experience a meaningful celibacy. Again, the choice between both these forms of life is a question of vocation, not of talent, greater perfection, or more radical effort. The surest sign of having been called to something is the bitter taste inevitably left behind by any later "rectification" made on one's own initiative. Anyone who has once felt the happiness of the life-path that is properly his or her own never finds real joy along an "alternative" path.

The classical distinction between "active" and "contemplative" vocations is often misleading too. *No* form of Christian life is even imaginable unless it would be at once *both* active and contemplative. No Christian, not even a Trappist, is called to a life of pure contemplation, while the most active Jesuit would be fundamentally unfaithful to his vocation were he to neglect contemplative prayer in the name of pressing apostolic activities. What Church law labels as "contemplative" is a group of people for whom prayer takes on a distinct, communal *form* and whose necessary and often extremely extensive work is not directly apostolically oriented (something that Church work very seldom is, for that matter).

Every Christian has to be active, whether that means caring for the sick, teaching children, or brewing beer. The form that activity will take, however, is a question of vocation. Every Christian has to pray, whether the form of prayer most typically happens to be sung prayer in the choir or individual meditation. The form of contemplative life, once again, depends upon the individual's specific vocation.

In the eyes of Ignatius, a Christian worthy of the name will always need to be *contemplativus in actione,* a contemplative in action. The distinction made by Church law between the various orders, then, consists in the *forms* assumed by this action and contemplation respectively. Within the various orders, work and prayer are "ordered" and structured in ways proper to each. Work in the fields is not less valuable, nor any less "active," than missionary work if God has called a certain person to this form of religious life. If what I do and how I pray is to have any value in God's sight, then it must depend on God's inspiration and not on the world's appreciation of it.

Diversity with respect to vocation concerns not only the various states of life possible, but the degree of intimacy with God to which a person may be called. This degree of intimacy does not depend upon one's personal merits, and still less upon one's juridical status. It is not necessarily the most impeccable people, not even monks and nuns, whom God calls most closely to himself. God calls whom he wills when he wills, and calls them as closely to himself as he wills.

The rich young man in the Gospel was offered a more intimate life together with the Lord: "Come, follow me" (Mk 10:21). Dismayed and disconcerted, he rejected the offer. It was, of course, not an *obligation:* like everyone else, he is obliged only to morality: "You know the commandments . . ." (Mk 10:9). In sharp contrast with him, there was another young man who proposed of *his own volition* to stay in the immediate proximity of the Lord: "As he was getting into the boat, the man . . . begged him that he might be with him. But (the Lord) refused and said to him, 'Go home to your friends . . .' " (Mk 5:18–19). The Lord's dismissal of him clearly demonstrates the gravity of his saying: "You did not choose me (on the basis of talent, personal preference, or noble-mindedness) but I chose you" (Jn 15:16).

Here we have, clearly expressed, an *in*equality in the matter of vocation. Just as all genuine love is gratuitous and unmerited, so also God's election is logically inexplicable. "My son, beware thou dispute not of high matters, nor of the secret judgments of God, why this man is so left, and that man taken into such great favor; why also one is so grievously afflicted, and another so eminently exalted. These things go beyond all reach of man's power, neither doth any reason or disputation avail to search out the judgments of God."[20]

In other words, there are no human criteria such as merits, efficiency, or natural talent which would enable us to understand the "why" of various vocations. Vocation finds its origin in the mystery of God's free love. "What is that to you?" Christ reproved Peter, when he asked why John, who was just another apostle, was allotted a destiny different from his (Jn 21:23). Here was an inequality which implied no injustice. "When . . . some curious persons raise the question, let thy answer be that of the prophet: 'Just art thou, O Lord, and right is thy judgment'

(Ps 118:137)."[21] There could be a question of injustice only if the one selected for greater intimacy would be allotted at the same time an easier path of life. But the inverse is true. Those who are called to more also stand closer to the cross of Christ.

For Christians, living in closer intimacy with God always means "being made like unto Christ." That includes being like the suffering, crucified Christ as well. To these more than to average Christians this word of Gerlach Peters applies: "For our whole life is a cross and must be a cross; only he who has experienced it knows how sweet it is."[22] Only one who accepts the cross that God has laid upon his or her shoulders, and all crosses like all graces are unequal, knows that this kind of suffering can mean budding happiness.

Is this some form of sublimated masochism? A masochist is someone who perversely cultivates personal suffering and takes pleasure in it, begging for attention and sympathy for his or her "poor" self. In Christian suffering, the opposite is true. The cross is not sought; it comes over a person. According to Peters, the cross always means a detachment from the self. What used to be my exclusive property is now laid open for the Other. God "breaks into" my heart. He can make an entrance into my "private domain" only after he himself has first broken down the egocentric walls around it.

A person thus "dis-appropriated" has the choice between self-enclosed, disappointed bitterness on the one hand and the counsel of the psalmist on the other: "Cast all your cares upon the Lord." Anyone choosing the latter course *is* immediately closer to the Lord. It is through one's very cares, anxieties and pains that one is touched. In a word: it is through one's cross. The cross, then, gradually brings a person where he or she originally did not wish to go: that is, toward surrender ("Into your hands, Father, I commend my spirit"). It is only after the confrontation with this cross that one can say of God's word within the self: "It is finished." Solitary selfishness is transformed through the cross into confident dependence on him who calls one to the Light, via Calvary.

A person's degree of intimacy with God does not depend upon any special juridical status. It is possible for a homemaker to experience closer contact with God than a cloistered nun. Therefore, within any state of life whatsoever, a person can be called to an especially graced prayer-life. Just as we do not expect the same intellectual or work life of everybody, we should not expect the same prayer life either. What is expected of everyone is a moral life: "If you would enter life, keep the commandments" (Mt 19:17). But some are called to "more." This "more" is no longer a question of obligation, commandment, or requirement. It is a matter of invitation, suggestion, counsel. Refusal of such a special vocation no longer has anything to do with sin or moral imperfection.

A servant is expected to carry out assigned duties carefully. Failure to fulfill that expectation is reprehensible. But from a friend, the only thing expected is, simply, friendship. For that, a person can only invite, not obligate. If I offer someone my special affection and that person clearly refuses it, then I cannot accuse that person of doing anything wrong. And yet this refusal will strike me as being more painful than the fact that my faithful servant would have shamefully neglected the duties I assigned. An ex-friend who is coolly "correct" toward me hurts me more and affects me more deeply than a sloppy servant. Being chosen for friendship is not on the level of duty but on the level of vocation. The "distressed and sad" departure of the rich young man seemed to have disappointed the Lord more painfully than the "many sins" of the woman who was "reckoned in the city as a sinner" but who "loved much" (cf. Lk 7:37 and 47).

Now, what is the content of such an election to greater intimacy with God? Ignatius speaks of greater "familiarity with God" ("familiaritas cum Deo") and of a life-style which is more

clearly in conformity with that of the Jesus of the Gospels. Ruusbroec speaks of "a loving interior adherence to God" and "a
ready willingness to let go of everything that one might possess
with desire and love apart from God."[23]

Ultimately, the distinction between the "servants" of God
and God's "chosen friends" lies more in the intensity of the experience. Among the "friends," conscious desire, hunger and
thirst for God are more strongly present. Levinas has phenomenologically described the human experience of God as a "desire
which cannot be satisfied." Speaking of this "metaphysical desire," he says that those who experience it are never satisfied by
the Beloved, but, on the contrary, they move ever more intensely toward desire: "The One Desired does not fill him but hol-
lows him out." It can be said of the religious person that "he
feeds on his hunger."[24] The person lives from this hunger for
God. The person's happiness consists in this hungry desire.

To experience God is to long for God. For that matter, desire is the core of all love. What else is the experience of love but
to know an intense, insatiable desire? The Christian mystics
have repeatedly contended that loving God always becomes a
"passion," that is, a suffering on account of the Other. It becomes a nostalgia for our true "fatherland," or feeling, as Ruusbroec put it, "ex-patriated," and experiencing a steadily
increasing longing for our true home, for the "Father's house"
with his "many mansions."

Since the relationship with God, insofar as it is experienced
consciously and psychologically, consists in insatiable longing,
then it is evident that there would be various degrees of intensity in it. There are people who do not even suspect what they are
missing. There are people who have never been "in love," who
have been blinded by countless snares of passing things which
do indeed satisfy but which leave a bitter aftertaste of "Is that all
there is?" But one who has been seized by God is never satisfied.
The passionate longing for the Beloved forms the very core of

one's happiness. This is a beatitude which is exactly the opposite of the Buddhist Nirvana. The Buddhist's "heaven" consists precisely in the *relinquishing* of all desires and passions, whereas the Christian speaks of insatiable passion.

The great Christian mystics of the thirteenth and sixteenth centuries, Hadewych of Antwerp, Beatrice of Nazareth, Teresa of Avila, John of the Cross, all of them literary masters, eagerly made use of erotic language and images inherited from the twelfth century Minnesingers. In fact, we know that these troubadours of Provence sang of a platonically-inspired "eros": "a desire that never relapses, that nothing can satisfy, that even rejects and flees the temptation to obtain its fulfillment in the world, because its demand is to embrace no less than the All."[25] Denis de Rougemont has shown that the erotic terminology of the minstrels had its origin in the religious language of the Catharist sect. As a consequence, medieval mysticism from the thirteenth century on brought back the originally religious, Catharist terms, later applied by the troubadours in a figurative sense to human eroticism (and not vice versa!), to their point of origin, namely, the relationship between human beings and God.[26]

For mysticism as well as for the lyricism of the Minnesingers and nearly all Western love literatures since then, what stands as central is hunger and thirst for the Beloved. In fact, for the believer, God is still the Incomprehensible. Anyone who may once have tasted something of his presence becomes increasingly fascinated by his mysterious attraction. Although God, in his revelation, comes to us in order to begin a love story with him, yet it is not in such a way as to remove or to bridge all distance between the two. The Divine and the human never flow together into a single totality. Where God "touches" a person, there arises a loving ardor of passionate desire for him, never a passionless rest.

The troubadour, too, in his own way sings of the "inaccessible." For this reason and this reason only, he draws so heavily on mystical terminology. His theme, and the basic theme of almost all Western literature, is always the same: the "great love" which arises outside an existing marriage and which is therefore impossible. What it recommends is never blessed possession but unrequited desire, not safe rest but a dangerous passion which stakes all and which occasionally, as in Tristan and Isolde, or in Romeo and Juliet, ends in death. Mysticism and erotic lyricism have only one point in common: both hanker after the "Inaccessible," and it is this passionate longing itself which is the basis of their only happiness. One, however, leads to full Life, the other via wild passion to a tragic death.

For the one who is called, then, the greater the religious hunger, the more conscious the feelings of love. Ruusbroec is convinced that the intimacy with God that people can arrive at, in this life as well as in heaven, is fundamentally unequal. The difference lies in the intensity of one's desire or spiritual hunger. "For the loveliest and noblest thing that God ever created in heaven and on earth is order and distinction among all creatures. . . . In this way, each is close to God and dependent upon him in greater or lesser degree; insofar as he hungers and thirsts and longs for God, to that degree he can experience, savor, and enjoy God. . . . Just as the stars in heaven differ in brilliance, in height, and in size . . . so also is there a distinction among all who love God."[27]

The more space or "emptiness" God finds in a person's heart, the more he can fill this heart with the abundance of his presence, but never, not even in eternity, to such a point that the heart would arrive at satisfaction and, as a result, lose its "hungry outlook," the core of its happiness. "For its part the loving soul is extraordinarily greedy and gluttonous, and it holds its desires wide open and wants to have everything that is shown to it. But it is creature and can neither swallow nor encompass the totality of God. And therefore it begins to have a great longing and desire, and to remain eternally thirsty and hungry. And the more it longs and desires, the more vividly it feels that God's riches pass it by. And this is called craving in want."[28]

It is only in this light that we can understand the meaning of the medieval concept of "purgatory" or "purifying fire after death." The eternal contemplation of God can mean only a constant experience of happiness for one whose eye has learned to see. Some people have already learned here on earth to distinguish the essential from the accidental. They are also more *capax Dei* (receptive for God) than others. In Catholic terminology they are called "saints." Immediately after their death, they are already in a condition to experience that for which they were created: to know God "face to face" (1 Cor 13:12).

The decisive import of earthly life lies in gradually learning to develop an eye for the Beautiful and Beatific. It is noteworthy that this process of learning or of purification ordinarily passes along the way of the cross. Life and its non-accidental vicissitudes either make a person ripe for lasting joy or else lay the groundwork for bitter despair. The degree of beatitude that "God has prepared for those who love him" (1 Cor 2:9), then, is measured by the "taste" for the "genuine" which a person has already cultivated on earth. The more one has an eye for the essential, the more passionately one will hunger and thirst for God already here on earth, and the more intense the beatitude of one's eternal happiness will be. Meanwhile, the godless person does not as yet realize what is being missed, and the superficial person still cannot succeed in getting "oriented." To apply the etymological meaning of the term "oriented," this latter person does not know how to turn east toward the Orient where the Eternal Light arises. In both of these cases then, purgatory or purification is still necessary.

Conclusion:
The Integral Humanism
of the Christian

Anyone who lets nature follow its course knows that every kitten will grow into a full-grown cat without fail, and a puppy into nothing less than a full-grown dog. In contrast, it is a much more complex affair to become fully human. An infant never grows up "on its own" into a human person. Here it does not suffice merely to leave nature alone. "Humanity" in fact presupposes a dose of culture.

It does not make sense to speak of an "un-horsey" horse. We do not even have a word for it; such imaginative fancies do not even come to mind. But a human being, on the other hand, can be "inhuman," can act "unhumanly" or remain "subhuman." This is why zeal for more "humanism" is meaningful. Many of those "created after the image of God" barely manage a few steps along the way to the goal of this difficult task. People who are immature, perverted, undeveloped, or infantile are, alas, no rarity.

In Christian terms, one is to be called a success only when, through the vicissitudes of life, one has become "human," *fully* human. "Gloria Dei vivens homo; the glory of God is a person fully alive," as Irenaeus said. God's glory consists in the fact that there are people who really "live" and are happy. What the Creator had in mind for us is that we would avail ourselves of the

187

nonaccidental life events we experience in order to grow into a human being. This growth is never the spontaneous result of the laws of nature; it is a vocation.

Christianity is the religion of "incarnation." Christianity is a humanism, but a humanism which strives to be "integral." Therefore, it refuses to make peace with the many contemporary forms of "cheap humanism" which are limited to biological, psychological, and political processes of development. The Christian humanist knows that humans are basically "religious" beings "created unto God," as Augustine says. Therefore, a Christian rejects any mutilated sort of "humanism" which does not reflect what it is to be human at its deepest dimensions. Reliance on these forms of "cheap humanism" justifiably leads to fears that their superficial methods of perception will interfere with gaining any grasp on these deeper regions. The Christian humanist knows that human beings by nature crave the Unfathomable and that a person's humanity is lacking and remains incomplete as long as that person has no feeling for the Infinite. When one does have it, it is then that the real "path of life" begins. Then one has started down the road to integral humanism.

As a matter of fact, all of creation is, in Teilhard's words, "a process of hominization." This is not a purely spiritual, interior happening. It is a cosmic event that involves nature and matter. A Christian is not someone who engages in self-"mortification." A Christian is one who "lives" life to the full knowing that one's highest desires can come forth only when the lowest impulses are held in "humane" check. Far from truncating, repressing, or disdaining "human nature" in the name of some falsely understood "supernatural" or "purely spiritual" values, a Christian gratefully receives material nature or bodiliness as a gift of God. The Christian sees in this gift the point of departure, willed and given by God, and the necessary baggage of his or her vocational history. It is the Christian's task to ennoble the natural elements, that is, to give them a form through culture.

In order to become a Christian, one must first become a human. God cannot make Christians out of sub-human beings, inhuman ascetics, or cultureless illuminati. It is not without reason that education, care of the sick, and help for economic development have always preceded genuine missionary work. What medieval Cistercians did in neglected regions of Europe, Father Lievens did in nineteenth century India: import agricultural techniques and social organization for the people, enhancing their humanity in order *afterward* to consecrate them in the sacramental life. People do not set a roof over chaotic emptiness. You can make a chimpanzee wet, but you cannot baptize it. A person and *only* a person can be ennobled into a genuine Christian by baptismal water. Sacraments presuppose humanity.

Without a humanity bedecked with culture, union with God is excluded. History teaches us that it is not superfluous to emphasize this. How often is not humanism trodden underfoot in the name of humility, poverty, or any other supernatural value? Symptomatic of this is the serious fact that Christians themselves start to attribute to unbelievers honorary titles such as "free-thinkers" or "humanists," as though anyone was called to greater freedom than the Christian, especially the Christian who understands his or her vocation correctly! Has not humanism been a typically Christian phenomenon for the very reason that the believer knows better than anyone else that anyone who disdains the nature of God is unworthy of the grace of God's supernature? *Gratia supponit naturam:* Grace builds on and presupposes nature. The life of faith glories in human culture. Creation and incarnation intersect. Manichaeans as well as the Albigensians of old were condemned as heretics by the Church. Christ's activity consists neither in saving "the good spirit" from "evil matter," nor in saving the "noble soul" from an "impure body."

It seems that the mystics have felt the value of what is integrally human more clearly than the majority of the Church.

Many a medieval nun or Beguine, probably the last ones people expected it from, repeatedly emphasized the necessity of a cultured humanism. Just like her contemporary Hadewych (ca. 1250), Beatrice of Nazareth (1268) refused to accept any dualism between natural intelligence and supernatural faith or community with God. Those wanting to approach God *must* use their intelligence, their affective life, and all their natural faculties. Supernature does not replace nature but builds upon it. Faith does not replace rational thought, but challenges and presupposes it.

These women, like all the "greats" of Christian mysticism, set themselves in opposition to any form of "spiritual life" which would debilitate the intellect or consider it superfluous. In contrast to the syrupy devotional literature of their time, they advocated a piety which included natural reason as well as affective experience of love. Emphasizing the nobility and greatness of human nature, these mystics were the forerunners of well-known Christian humanists such Pico de la Mirandola, Thomas More, and Erasmus.

With a distinct guilt-feeling for undervaluing her natural talents (her *bona naturalia*) in youth, Beatrice writes in her autobiography that letting them lie fallow had stilted her spiritual life.[1] It seemed to her "of utmost necessity that with all her strength she should learn to conform herself to the purity of nature. Furthermore, in order to reach this perfection, she would have to reorient herself with all the necessary effort of her affective life, and, as to the rest, exercise herself in this crystalline purity as much as the grace for it should be accorded her." As was the case for all the great figures of medieval spirituality, nature in her eyes was essentially good. For nature was God's gift and God's creation. True, sin makes nature go off the track God intended for it. But grace gives a person the possibility "to restore his supernatural powers and virtues, and, in so doing, to bring the purity of nature back to its original state."[2]

For an intellectual artist such as Hadewych too, lucid understanding is the necessary prerequisite for any life of union with God. Warning her friend against an un-Christian, false humility, she says that it is her religious duty to make use of all her natural talents and to further develop them. "For before God you are obliged to take cognizance of all the good that you could achieve with effort, by questioning, study, and serious application."[3]

True humility, says Hadewych later on, is shown by the one who wants to become what God wills for him or her. You are humble only when you lift yourself above all that is less than God himself "in the totality of your nature."[4] God does not allow the amputation of so-called superfluous natural gifts in the name of pure love of God. A Christian is never called to self-mutilation. For God wants to be found and loved by the whole person in "forthright pride" and in "nobility of nature."

Seen in the context of her times, Hadewych's statement that a person can come to a union with God in love by the right use of rational powers and not by moderating normal affective outpourings,[5] meaning that religion does not exclude reason but on the contrary implies it, was a strikingly new sound and an almost revolutionary thought. In fact, we must not forget that in the twelfth century the West had rediscovered pagan Greco-Arabian thought initially inspired by Aristotle. Theologians of those times correctly felt that these new logical thought processes were an outright challenge addressed to them. A group of them, among whom there are great names such as Bernard or Richard of St. Victor, chose the simplest solution: they rejected the Aristotelian approach which they deemed harmful and adhered to a life of piety that refused the whole problematic of philosophical thought.

So Christian spirituality engaged in a flight to the mountains of mysticism, while reason was left behind in the despised, even feared, valley of the world's thought and discussion. A string of other theologians would retreat for security to the Orientally inspired writings of Dionysius the Areopagite and his "negative theology" which saw God as inaccessible and unknowable by reason: we can only "feel" him with the heart and adhere to him fideistically. Such a split between supernatural faith and natural thought, an unbearable one for a humanist, is rejected by mystics like Hadewych and William of Saint-Thierry in an almost revolutionary way. In their eyes, piety cannot be a reserve for the underdeveloped where they would be protected from intellectual thought. On the contrary, Christian piety presupposes a maximum development of everyone's human faculties. In other words, mature faith requires a balanced humanism. A theological school should not be a sheltered workshop. At the root of this openness to the world lies the conviction that there can be no contradiction or incompatibility between the two gifts of God, reason and faith.

The thought that one must first develop and exercise his or her natural gifts no matter how modest these may be (even a single talent may not be hidden in the ground) if one intends to reckon on God's free grace belongs to the very essence of Christianity. It is then by no means a question of a clever but contingent discovery by a few medieval pious persons in the course of Church history; however, it has seemed necessary again and again to emphasize with new urgency and convincing arguments the role of humanism, the irreplaceable value of human nature as well as human culture.

Every Christian "Renaissance" movement and even every renewal inspired by an individual Christian genius (e.g., Nicholas of Cusa, Erasmus, or Teilhard) began with a defense of integral humanism as the irreplaceable foundation. Even an eremitical mystic such as Ruusbroec clearly understood this when, speaking of "supernatural faith," he stated that "those who want to receive it . . . must bring nature to the highest point that nature can attain." Only when a person's nature has been brought to the highest level that the person's talents can reach does the proper task of supernature or of grace begin. "When nature is insufficient and can proceed no farther, then God comes with supernatural light and illuminates the understanding, so that this person believes and hopes more than we can describe." Grace interacts with nature and fulfills it. "When a person does what he can and can go no farther on account of his own infirmity, then it belongs to the fathomless goodness of God to complete that work."[7]

We can scarcely formulate the essence of Christianity more pithily than the way Ruusbroec phrased it: "practicing love" between God and human beings and, modeled on that, between individual human beings and their "neighbors." Love worthy of the name always includes two phases: the partners *give* to each other, and they *receive* from each other. The high regard for the human person which has always characterized genuine Christianity nowhere appears so clearly as in the Christian conviction that God does not one-sidedly give to human beings. God gives us the capacity to *give him* something in return, something very valuable even in his sight.

We are made to be free, creative persons. It is impossible to have perfect love between two parties, one of whom is giving and the other asking, or purely receptive. A true love relationship is not a "charitable organization"; love rules out one-way traffic. Total inequality makes partnership impossible. However strange it may sound to the ears of a pious pagan, a human person has a marvelous dignity in the sight of God. As the old Latin liturgy phrased it: "God, who created human nature in wondrous dignity and even more wonderfully (by his incarnation) renewed it . . ."

Humankind, therefore, is willed and created by God as the *center* of the creation event, not as the top of the pyramid of evolving matter. Standing between God and matter, the human person is a priest who gives human form to chaotic matter by using and working on it in order to give it back to its Creator. The

Christian should ennoble matter and corporeality rather than disdain or flee from them. In contrast to many other great religions, the Christian regards matter not as a danger, an illusion, or a handicap, but rather as a task and even as a challenge. The same theme is found in Teilhard de Chardin's essay "The Mass on the World." In the world the clear traces of the Creator's hand can be discovered. It is the human task to "subdue" the earth (Gn 1:28), to "master matter and so be able to attain and submit to the light of God."[8]

Created matter is the locus willed by God for his human creatures, the place to which God calls us in order to encounter him, and, consequently, the place where God has his "rendezvous" with us. We can hardly imagine any greater attribution of worth to matter than we find in Christianity. Here matter is not the lower section of a two-stage rocket, meant to fly off and be lost in nothingness as soon as the human *soul* would reach God's eternity. Rather, matter is the irreplaceable instrument with which we are to become more human and by aid of which we are to try to live in ever greater human dignity. The material world is more than a means; or, to put it in Abraham Heschel's words: "The world is an allusion," characterized by "a spiritual suggestiveness and an allusiveness to transcendent meaning."[9] Matter has an irreplaceable role in the growth of humankind toward an integral humanism.

Surely when God creates he is concerned only with humanity. "For it is a question of man, in his human presence," according to the poet Saint-John Perse. But Perse is referring to "man" as interwoven with the entire cosmos, "man" who is never to be thought of as an abstraction apart from the matter in which human origins, history and future expectations have their roots.

For centuries of cultural history human beings have worked with matter in an effort to make it, "to re-create" it, into a temple for the ultimate encounter with God. There is certainly reason for hope for matter itself, "for creation itself will be set free

from its bondage to decay" (Rom 8:21). To put it in the words
of the Christian poet Gezelle:

> God! I alone [i.e., the individual man or woman] am your
>   priest on earth,
> For me Thy creation is a temple
> And Thou, O God, willest to receive
> All created things from my hands.
> I am king of all about me
> And all about me, Thou madest it, Thou gavest
> It to me, to give it back to Thee.
> And yet—O mystery of God!—if I give it not
> Thou leavest it and it is lost to Thee.[10]

Notes

Introduction
1. Cf. Saul Bellow, *Mr. Sammler's Planet* (London, 1972), p. 5.
2. A. Vauchez, *La Spiritualité du Moyen Age occidental* (Paris, 1975), p. 158.
3. R. D. Laing, *The Politics of Experience* (New York, 1967), p. 20.
4. Harvey Cox, *The Feast of Fools* (Cambridge, Mass., 1969), pp. 14–15.
5. Emmanuel Lévinas, *Totalité et Infini* (The Hague, 1971), p. 33.
6. *Ibid.*, pp. 21 and 34.
7. Jacques Ellul, *The New Demons,* trans. C. E. Hopkin (New York, 1975), pp. 26 and 158.
8. Laing, *Politics,* pp. 25–26.

Chapter One
1. F. Alquié, *L'Experience* (Paris, 1970), pp. 20 and 5.
2. P. Tillich, *The New Being* (London, 1956), pp. 129–130.
3. H. Miller, *Plexus* (New York, 1965), p. 88.
4. Denis de Rougemont, *Love and the Western World,* trans. M. Belgion (New York, 1940), p. 53.
5. T. Roszak, *The Making of a Counter Culture* (New York, 1968), p. 236.
6. P. Tillich, *Trennung und Einigung im Erkenntnisakt,* Gesammelte Werke, IV (Stuttgart, 1961), p. 112.
7. A. H. Maslow, *Motivation and Personality* (New York, 1954), pp. 147 and 148.
8. A. Nin, *The Journals of Anaïs Nin II, 1934–1939* (London, 1967), p. 255.
9. J. H. Newman, *Lectures on the Present Position of Catholics in England* (Dublin, 1857), pp. 260–261.

Chapter Two
1. E. Fromm, *Marx, Freud, en de Vrijheid, de Bevrijding van de Mens uit de Ketenen der Illusies* (Utrecht, 1970), p. 119.
2. H. Van den Berg, *Wat is Psychotherapie?* (Nijkerk, 1970), p. 39.
3. V. Frankl, *La Psychothérapie et son Image de l'Homme* (Paris, 1970), pp. 149–150.
4. V. Frankl, *The Doctor and the Soul* (New York, 1969), p. 220.
5. P. Berger, *Invitation to Sociology. A Humanistic Perspective.* (London, 1968), p. 78.
6. D. Bonhoeffer, *Letters and Papers from Prison* (New York, 1967), pp. 30–31.
7. H. Bergson, *The Two Sources of Morality and Religion,* trans. R. Ashley (Garden City, 1935), p. 80.

Chapter Three
1. Saint-John Perse, *Vents* (Paris, 1960), pp. 88–89.
2. H. Bergson, *The Two Sources of Morality and Religion* (New York, 1935), p. 34.
3. A. Gehlen, *Die Seele im technischen Zeitalter* (Hamburg, 1957), p. 116.
4. J. Baruzi, *Saint Jean de la Croix et le Problème de l'Expérience mystique* (Paris, 1924), pp. 217–218.
5. W. James to H. Leuba, 17/4/1904, in *The Letters of William James* (New York, 1969), p. 211.
6. I. Illich, *Celebration of Awareness: A Call for Institutional Revolution* (New York, 1970), p. 11.
7. P. de Grandmaison, *La Religion personnelle* (Paris, 1927), p. 178.
8. Jan van Ruusbroec, *Werken I,* ed. Ruusbroec-Genootschap (Tielt, 1944), pp. 239 and 180.
9. P. Debongnie, *La grande Dame du pur Amour, Sainte Catherine de Gênes* (Bruges, 1960), p. 36.
10. Cf. J. Ellul, *The New Demons* (New York, 1975); T. Luckmann, *The Invisible Religion* (New York, 1967).
11. H. Bergson, *op. cit.,* p. 274.

Chapter Four
1. D. de Rougemont, *Love and the Western World* (Paris, 1940), p. 89.
2. Hadewych, *Strofische Gedichten,* ed. Rombauts and De Paepe (Zwolle, 1961), p. 116.

3. St. Thérèse of Lisieux, *Story of a Soul,* trans. J. Clarke (Washington, 1975), pp. 210, 214.

4. J. Baudrillard, *La Société de Consommation* (Paris, 1970), pp. 112–113.

5. D. de Rougemont, *Love and the Western World,* p. 33.

6. J. de Bourbon-Busset, *Complices, Journal V* (Paris, 1974), p. 187.

7. D. de Rougemont, *Penser avec les Mains* (Paris, 1972), p. 158.

8. E. Lévinas, *Totalité et Infini* (The Hague, 1971), p. 13.

9. In C. Chabanis, *Dieu existe-t-il? Non* (Paris, 1973), p. 332.

10. Cf. Jn 14:27; 16:1; 13:19; 14:29; 16:4.

11. John of the Cross makes a distinction between the "night of the senses" and the "night of the soul." This second night, which is already a strictly mystical unitive experience, will remain outside the scope of our consideration here. "The night of the senses is common and happens to many. The spiritual night is the lot of very few, of those who have been tried and are proficient," according to John of the Cross, *Dark Night,* Book I, Chapter 8. *The Collected Works,* trans. K. Kavanaugh, O.C.D. (Washington, 1973), p. 97.

12. John of the Cross, *op. cit.,* I, Chapters 10 and 9, pp. 316 and 311.

13. D. de Rougemont, *Love and the Western World,* p. 265.

14. Sartre defines masochism as "a perpetual effort to annihilate the subjectivity of the subject by making it get reassimilated by the other, and this effort is accompanied by the exhausting and delicious awareness of failure": cf. J.-P. Sartre, *L'Etre et le Néant* (Paris, 1943), p. 447. Delightful loss of one's own subjectivity in the Other is a well-known pattern in Eastern religions.

15. M. Clavel, *Ce que je crois* (Paris, 1975), p. 21.

Chapter Five

1. E. Benveniste has, in fact, demonstrated that Cicero, and not Lactantius, was right when the former read the stem *legere* rather than *ligari* in the word *religio.* Originally *religere* meant the opposite of *negligere* (to neglect). Then *religio* becomes a reassumption, a retracing of one's steps, the remaking of a choice. In this context, then, religious man was rather a hesitant, scrupulous person. Cf. E. Benveniste, *Le Vocabulaire des Institutions Indo-européennes* II (Paris, 1969), pp. 265–272.

2. F. Alquié, *L'Expérience* (Paris, 1970), p. 110.

3. "There are certainly reasons for keeping silent about God. We

speak to facilely about him. Theologians have even summed up all the categories of God's own knowledge, spiritual leaders of the old style tell us precisely what God's will is, and leaders from new movements do the same. We were too little aware that for St. Thomas himself the last word about our knowledge of God is to know that we do not know him. Today we have become sensitive for the Buddha's silence, the 'neti, neti' of the Hindus, the negative or apophatic theologians of the East and their roots in the Scriptures. This is a gain, on one condition. The condition is that, just as we heard from St. Thomas, silence comes last, not first. If we begin by keeping silence, then we 'silence' God to death": P. Schoonenberg in his farewell address, "Thinking unto God" (*Denken naar God toe*).

4. R. Laing, *The Politics of Experience* p. 35.

5. Guillevic, *Carnac* (Paris, 1961), Stanzas 13, 17, and 18.

6. "There is no reality, thing or event which cannot become a bearer of the mystery of being and enter into a revelatory correlation": P. Tillich, *Systematic Theology* I (London, 1951), p. 131.

7. E. Ionesco, *Journal en Miettes*, Paris, 1967, p. 45.

8. Cf. A. H. Maslow, *Religious Values and Peak-Experiences* (Ohio, 1964), and R. C. Zaehner, *Mysticism, Sacred and Profane* (Oxford, 1957).

9. Jan van Ruusbroec, *Die Geestelike Brulocht*, in *Werken* I, pp. 228–229.

10. Samyntta Nikaya, in E. J. Thomas, *Early Buddhist Scriptures* (London, 1935), pp. 117–118.

11. Ruusbroec, *Die Geestelike Brulocht* I, pp. 228–237.

12. Marcel Proust, *Remembrance of Things Past* (New York, 1956), p. 62 (italics ours).

13. William James, *The Varieties of Religious Experience* (New York, 1961), p. 310, n. 12.

14. A. Rimbaud, *A Season in Hell* (Connecticut, 1945), pp. 13, 71, 87, 89. Cf. also Zaehner, *Mysticism, Sacred and Profane*, pp. 61–83.

15. P. Teilhard de Chardin, *The Phenomenon of Man* (New York, 1959), p. 209.

16. *Bhagavad-Gita* (New York, 1968), XVIII, nos. 53, 54, 55, 64, 65, pp. 137–138.

17. *Sayings of Sri Ramakrishna* (Madras, 1949), p. 320.

18. R. C. Zaehner, *Hinduism* (London, 1966), p. 10.

19. A Chinese Zen-Master, cited by Marghanita Laski, in *Ecstasy: A Study of Some Secular and Religious Experiences* (London, 1961), p. 54, n. 1.

Chapter Six

1. J. Moltmann, Mensch, *Christliche Anthropologie in den Konflikten der Gegenwart* (Stuttgart, 1971), p. 121.

2. Denis de Rougemont, *The Myths of Love* (New York, 1961), p. 207.

3. Richard de Saint-Victor, *De Trinitate*, 3, XIV.

4. E. Benveniste, *Problèmes de Linguistique générale* (Paris, 1966), pp. 253, 259, and 260.

5. "Man is absolutely not a thing, but a drama. . . . Man is the novelist—whether original or plagiarist—of himself": Ortega y Gasset, *Historie als Systeem,* cited by J. H. Walgrave, *Geloof en Theologie in de Crisis* (Kasterlee, 1966), p. 67. "Man . . . is made by history. History is man in the making. He does not have a history, he *is* history. History . . . as a whole is an anthropogony, that is, a tale of incarnation, of becoming man": Walgrave, *ibid.*

6. R. Barthes, *Fragments d'un Discours amoureux* (Paris, 1977), p. 162.

7. In modern Dutch jargon, people here would speak of "making a relationship true" (*waarmaken*). But it is an improper term, for the relationship *is* and remains true. It can only be made (more) conscious, gradually increasing in intimacy and leading to more radical consequences in my deeds and life-style.

8. K. Barth, *Die christliche Dogmatik im Entwurf,* pp. 295–297.

9. J. Moltmann, *Theology of Play,* trans. R. Ulrich (New York, 1972), p. 48.

10. J. Moltmann, *op. cit.,* p. 46.

11. E. Mounier, *Le Personnalisme* (Paris, 1965), p. 102.

12. F. M. Dostoyevsky, *The Brothers Karamazov* (New York, n.d.), pp. 282–285.

13. J. Moltmann, *Theology of Play,* pp. 47 and 48.

14. H. Hesse, *Steppenwolf,* trans. B. Creighton (New York, 1963), pp. 50–51.

15. A. Hellensberg, *Mystik der Gottesferne, Eine Interpretation Thomas Manns* (Bern-Munich, 1960), p. 9.

16. Thomas Mann, *Meine Zeit: Vortrag gehalten in der Universitat Chicago* (May, 1950).

17. J. Huizinga, *The Waning of the Middle Ages* (Garden City, 1954), pp. 264 and 152.

18. P. Tillich, *Der Protestantismus als Kritik und Gestaltung* (Munich, 1966), p. 139.

19. "The Church is cause and not result of personal piety. It is not a work of pious persons, but the pious persons are the product of the Church. . . . It is not the Christian's religious experience which creates the Church, but rather truth which forms the foundations of the church is the source of manifold religious experiences": P. Tillich, *ibid.*, p. 138.

20. "We are joined together, not by ceremonies but by the Spirit of Christ; anyone from whom his spirit is absent is alien to Christ" (Erasmus, *Paraphrases in Rom. 8, Opera VII*, p. 590). Cf. also: "Corporeal works are not condemned, but invisible ones are to be preferred. Visible worship is not condemned, but God is not pleased except by invisible piety" (Erasmus, *Encheiridion Militis Christiani*, 85, No. 20).

21. E. Lévinas, *Totalité et Infini*, p. 181.

Chapter Seven

1. Berger, *The Precarious Vision* (New York, 1961), p. 207.

2. E. Mounier, *Le Personnalisme* (Paris, 1965), p. 129.

3. W. H. Auden, *Genius and Apostle*, in *Selected Essays* (London, 1962), p. 206.

4. D. Hammarskjöld, *Markings*, trans. L. Sjöberg and W. H. Auden (New York, 1974), p. 19.

5. *Ibid.*, p. 66.

6. *Ibid.*, pp. 205–206.

7. P. and B. Berger, *Sociology: A Biographical Approach* (New York, 1975), p. 258.

8. Ruusbroec, *Werken*, II, p. 9.

9. J. Moltmann, *Theology of Play*, trans. R. Ulrich (New York, 1972), pp. 48–49.

10. Cf. Ruusbroec, *Werken*, II, p. 86.

11. J. Clemence, "Le Discernement des Esprits," in *Revue d'Ascétique et de Mystique*, 27 (1951), p. 375.

12. Ignatius of Loyola, *The Text of the Spiritual Exercises of St. Ignatius* (Westminster, n.d.), pp. 114, 112.

13. J. Clemence, "Le Discernement des Esprits," in *R.A.M.* (1952), p. 79.

14. ". . . per ratiocinationem et discursum securior et tutior." Cf. Monumenta Historica Societatis Jesu, Dict. S. pp. 269 (Mercurianus) and 699, 701, 707, 708, and 727 (Aquaviva).

15. Ionesco, in C. Chabanis, *Dieu existe-t-il? Non répondent . . .* (Paris: 1973), p. 334.

16. R. Schutz, "Un oui qui reste oui," in *Lutte et Contemplation, Journal 1970–1972* (Taizé, 1973), p. 23.

17. "... sine causa praecedente; without any preceding cause for it ... that is, without any previous perception or knowledge of any object from which such consolation might come to the soul, by means of its own acts of the understanding and will": Ignatius, *Spiritual Exercises,* pp. 111–112.

18. A. Deblaere, "Gerlach Peters (1378–1411), Mysticus van de 'Onderscheiding der Geesten,' " in *Liber Amicorum Prof. Dr. E. Rombauts* (Louvain, 1968), p. 99.

19. Cf. "Dossier Deliberación," Centrum Ignatianum Spiritualitatis (Rome, 1971).

20. Thomas a Kempis, *The Following of Christ,* Book III, Ch. 58, 1–2, trans. R. Challoner (New York, 1895).

21. *Ibid.,* Ch. 58, v. 3.

22. Gerlach Peters, *Soliloquium Ignitum cum Deo,* Chapter XII: "Tota vita nostra crux est et esse debet; quam dulcis sit, solus novit qui sentit."

23. Ruusbroec, *Werken,* III, p. 16.

24. E. Lévinas, *Totalité et Infini* (The Hague, 1971), pp. 3, 4, and 21.

25. D. de Rougemont, *Love and the Western World* (USA, 1940), p. 56.

26. Cf. H. Bergson: "When critics reproach mysticism with expressing itself in the same terms as passionate love, they forget that it was love which began by plagiarizing mysticism. ... In using the language of a passion it had transfigured, mysticism has only resumed possession of its own": *The Two Sources of Morality and Religion,* trans. R. A. Auda and C. Brereton (New York, 1935), p. 142.

27. Ruusbroec, *Werken,* III, p. 110.

28. Ruusbroec, *Werken,* III, pp. 214–215.

Conclusion

1. As "bona naturalia" Beatrice reports, *inter alia,* "naturalis decor animae," "profunditas cordis," "fertilitas naturae," subtilitas ingenii," "naturalis et nobilis superbia," "largitas, habilitas et affabilitas, etc." Cf. *Vita Beatricis, De Autobiografie van de Z. Beatrijs van Tienen,* ed. L. Reypens (Antwerp, 1964), pp. 86–88.

2. *Ibid.,* p. 88.

3. Hadewych, *Brieven,* ed. F. Van Bladel and B. Spaapen (Tielt, 1954), p. 229.

4. Cf. *ibid.,* p. 93.

5. For all of this, cf. A. Deblaere, "Hadewych," in *Twintig Eeuwen Vlaanderen,* Part 13, pp. 25–28 (Hasselt, 1976).

6. Ruusbroec, *Werken,* I, p. 25.

7. *Ibid.,* p. 108.

8. P. Teilhard de Chardin, "The Mass on the World," in *Hymn of the Universe* trans. S. Bartholomew (New York, 1965), p. 208.

9. Abraham J. Heschel, *Man Is Not Alone* (New York, 1976), pp. 12 and 22.

10. G. Gezelle, "O 'k sta mij zo geren," in *Volledige Dichtwerken* (Antwerp, 1971), pp. 335–336.